Envision Your Extraordinary Life

Living Happy, Joyous, and Free

Envision Your Extraordinary Life

Living Happy, Joyous, and Free

First Edition

By Linda M. Hogan
Linda M. Hogan Consulting

Envision Your Extraordinary Life

Living Happy, Joyous, and Free

This edition published by
Linda M Hogan Consulting
Glen Allen, VA
linda.hogan@envisionyourlife.coach

Copyright © 2021 by Linda M. Hogan Consulting.
All rights reserved.

No part of this book may be reproduced or transmitted in any form or by any means, electronic or mechanical, including photocopying, recording, or by any information storage and retrieval system, without written permission from the author, except for the inclusion of brief quotations in a review.

First Edition

Book Design and Illustrations: Mitch Sayers
Book Cover Design: Mitch Sayers
Editor: Spencer Iovoli
Photography: Bill Collins

Envision Your Extroardinary Life is a registered trademark of Linda M. Hogan Consulting

Want to learn more about *Envision Your Extraordinary Life*?
For more information and resources
scan the QR Code or
To go to the website:
https://www.envisionyourlife.coach

About Linda M. Hogan

Linda Hogan is grateful for her life exactly as it is right now. Linda led training at Fortune 100 companies in the US and Europe and has coached individuals to create and implement a compelling vision for success. She enjoys traveling in search of scenic beauty, laughing with her daughters, Sarah and Anna, and seeing Emmylou Harris in concert every chance she gets. Linda runs with her dog Kimo, drinks fabulously strong coffee, and enjoys fine dining at home in Virginia with her chef/husband Bill.

Disclaimer

This book is designed to provide information on helping an individual create an amazing life through goal setting and guided imagery. It is sold with the understanding that the author is not engaged in rendering mental health, legal, medical, or other professional services. If expert assistance is required, the services of a competent professional should be sought. Every effort has been made to make this book as complete and as accurate as possible. However, there may be mistakes, both typographical and in content. Therefore, this text should be used only as a general guide and not the ultimate source of information. Furthermore, this book contains information that is current only up to the publishing date. The purpose of this book is to educate and motivate. The author shall have neither liability nor responsibility to any person or entity with any loss or damage caused, or alleged to have been caused, directly or indirectly, by the information contained in this book.

Book Dedication

I dedicate this book to my amazing husband Bill Collins who has been with me through all the ups and downs of our lives over the past 48 years. You remind me of what is important and to not take myself so seriously. I am grateful for you, your support and sense of humor, and all the gourmet meals you make every day! I dedicate this book to my two daughters, Sarah and Anna, who have brought me so much joy and laughter. I am proud of who you are and the amazing lives you have created.

I am eternally grateful for the women who have walked with me on the road to recovery and who joined me as I experimented with guided imagery in numerous workshops and retreats for over 35 years. You know who you are! Your enthusiasm, support, and feedback inspired me and allowed me to hone my craft. You listened to your higher power and applied the principles we discussed; many of your stories are included in this book. I am grateful to all the men and women who have shared their stories! I have grown because of you.

Table of Contents

Table of Contents

	What People Say	12
	Introduction	15
	The Journey Together	16
Module 1	Creating a Vision	24
Module 2	Dream.	46
Module 3	Values, Mission, and Priorities	68
Module 4	Charting a Course.	90
Module 5	Achieving Your 90-day Goals	110
Module 6	Travel Light	130
Module 7	Overcoming Obstacles.	150
Module 8	Healing and Wellness	166
Module 9	Enhancing Skills and Performance. . .	186
Module 10	Boldly Follow Your Dreams	204
	Conclusion.	220
	End Notes	224

What People Say

Read this book if you want a picture and pathway to achieving serenity and your life's purpose. Working this program, I realized a spiritual transformation that was much deeper than just goal setting. I am now able to show up both professionally and personally in a more confident and self-assured way. I have a much clearer direction for my life.

> **Teri Lovelace, Esq**
> **Founder and Former President, LOCUS Impact Investing**
> **Glen Allen, Virgina**

Getting into the 'space' with you and the rest of the ladies in our group propelled my life in a direction I could have never dreamed of. My imagination was opened as a result of this course and I was able to really envision myself doing things I never thought possible. I stepped into a new way of being in the world that's still coming into focus for me to this day. The unexpected, residual effects of this course are still shaping me and moving me in directions yet unseen. I can feel the flow and I know that whatever is to come will be wonderful and full of joy. It's so hard to put my experience into words. For me it was both a beautiful and messy process at times. I think of that afternoon sitting on the floor of my condo crying and ripping out pages from magazines to create my vision board. Balling some of the pages up and throwing them across the room as I raged; cursing the gods and my ancestors, my own shortcomings, my ridiculous self-defeating patterns, and even my humanity at times... and, in the middle of that storm, there was healing happening—all at the same time. In the end, what I pasted to the back of an old Little Caesar's pizza box would hold a bold new vision for my future... a new and exciting chapter.

Forever thankful for such a beautiful experience—opened me up wide and ready for something new.

> **Brandi Brown**
> **Intuitive Life Coach**
> **Richmond, Virginia**

Read this book if you are entering a new phase of your life.

I was able to relax during the guided imageries and now focus more on the positive. New images and ideas for my future appeared. By writing down my goals and making steady progress, I have achieved positive outcomes in relationships, health, and finances. I have transitioned successfully from working full time to being retired and have been able to dedicate time to a non-profit organization.

Wanda Moser
Retired Human Resources Professional
Henrico, Virginia

The shift I wanted to create in my life was to set priorities, establish and meet my goals, and feel confident — I'm going in the right direction. As a result of the process described in this book, I feel more in control of my life, have met goals I never thought possible, and I'm living the life I've always dreamed of.

Deb Vanderpool
Registered Dietitian
Puerto Morelos, Mexico

Linda is inspiring and gifted. Her Visionary Mastermind Alliance workshops have helped me to reach goals I had always wanted to achieve, but lacked the roadmap and tools to get there. The guidance contained in this book can help anyone envision and achieve the things in life they desire.

Doreen Holland
Director, Claims Processing
Glen Allen, Virginia

In 1989, when I started to work with Linda Hogan, I could not write a single dream. Monumental changes have taken place in me and every aspect of my life. She gave me a structure that was easy to follow with a deeply spiritual approach. If you really want to change your life, read this book. Be prepared and it will be a wonderful experience!

Carolyn Lawrence
Owner, Hudson B&B
Hudson, NY

Introduction

Introduction

The purpose of this book is to take you on a journey to create a life worth living. My firm conviction is that we all have the power to create an amazing life. My hope is that you will envision, realize, and enjoy a life that is beyond your wildest expectations; a vision that will move you on your life path to be happy, joyous, and free. You deserve it!

Women with Vision — Happy, Joyous, and Free: The Beginning

Twelve women — different in many ways, we had little in common. We were single, divorced and married. We were white, black, and brown. We were young, old, and in between. We were housewives, businesswomen, social workers, educators, and students. We were daughters, we were mothers, and we were grandmothers. But we had that one thing that brought us together. We were alcoholics.

We came together once a month to create a better life for ourselves and to support one another through the process. We gathered to create a vision for our lives — a vision without alcohol or drugs, a vision for a life where God, not ego, is center stage. We imagined the possibilities, we listened to our hearts, and we acted. We stayed sober, we achieved results beyond our wildest expectations, and we created the lives we envisioned.

Caroline, an experienced educational administrator, left the pleasant confines of upstate New York and followed her passion to New York City to attend the New York School of Design. She opened an interior design business and bought and renovated a co-op on Manhattan's Upper East Side. Paulette, new to America and seeking something familiar in a foreign land, found an apartment in a rural mountain town that reminded her of her home in Switzerland. While realizing our vision, we all experienced the four paradoxes of recovery: our ego died so we could live; we let go to have power; we suffered to get well; and we surrendered to win.

> **All that we are is the result of what we have thought.**
>
> **— Buddha**

The Journey Together

> To laugh often and much; to win the respect of intelligent people and the affection of children; to earn the appreciation of honest critics and endure the betrayal of false friends; to appreciate beauty; to find the best in others; to leave the world a bit better, whether by a healthy child, a garden patch or a redeemed social condition; to know even one life has breathed easier because you have lived. This is to have succeeded.
>
> — Ralph Waldo Emerson

**Think about what Emerson said.
What does this mean to you?
How do you define success?**

Welcome — Let's get started. Join us in my kitchen. Grab a cup of coffee or tea, and a cookie or muffin. We will mingle for a bit and then move into my living room; find a comfy chair. We are all on this journey together. If you are reading this book alone, I encourage you to find at least one other person to take this journey with you, a small group is even better. Sharing the journey with others encourages, inspires, and helps us to be accountable for what we believe and plan to do. And, it's more fun. Let's talk about where you are now and where you would like to go. As a child, did you have a dream for yourself, a tiny spark, an inkling, an idea of who you would become? You are a painter creating your future. The world is your canvas and your choices are unlimited.

What was your childhood dream? See it in your mind. Draw or write a couple of words about it. What picture do you choose to create? Create a life beyond your wildest dreams!

At the end of this journey, you will be able to:

- Create a compelling vision for your future
- Generate a list of dreams
- Define your values, mission, and priorities
- Chart a course for your new path
- Travel lightly and deepen your spirituality
- Achieve 90-day goals
- Overcome obstacles and adversity
- Improve your health and healing
- Enhance skills and performance
- Boldly follow your dreams
- Realize your deepest desires

Your Goals for This Program

Write a description of your top three desired results. Remember to make your goals SMART!

S   **Specific** — See it in your mind's eye.

M   **Measurable** — Make it a game and keep score.

A   **Attainable** — Stretch to achieve.

R   **Relevant** — Align with what is important to you.

T   **Target Date** — Date it.

These don't need to be perfect right now, just jump in; we will improve it later.

My top three desired results — my three goals.

1	
2	
3	

Envisioning an Extraordinary Life — Assessment:

The Where I Am Right Now

Directions: For your own amazement and amusement, let's take a look at how you now use the tools and ideas we will discover and refine on our journey together. This will give you a better idea of the terrain we will explore. We will take this assessment again at the end of our journey, so that we can measure our growth. Read each statement and circle the number that best describe where you are right now.

The rating scale goes from 1, meaning strongly disagree, to 5, strongly agree.

1	2	3	4	5
Strongly Disagree	Slightly Disagree	Slightly agree	Agree	Strongly Agree

1.	I have an abundant supply of dreams — ideas for what my future can become.	1	2	3	4	5
2.	I have written and specific goals.	1	2	3	4	5
3.	I know what my mission/ purpose is in life.	1	2	3	4	5
4.	I have a identified my most important values and principles for living.	1	2	3	4	5
5.	My priority goals are based on my mission and values.	1	2	3	4	5
6.	I know what kind of legacy I want to leave behind.	1	2	3	4	5
7.	I find it easy to visualize the dreams I want to create in my life.	1	2	3	4	5
8.	I can vividly see myself already in possession of my goals.	1	2	3	4	5
9.	I have a strong desire to create the goals I want.	1	2	3	4	5
10.	I practice visualizing the goals I want in life.	1	2	3	4	5
11.	I regularly say affirmations that support the goals I want in life.	1	2	3	4	5
12.	I always follow my intuition.	1	2	3	4	5
13.	I have clearly identified the benefits to achieving my goals.	1	2	3	4	5
14.	I believe that I deserve the goals I want to achieve.	1	2	3	4	5
15.	I have a vision board to support my goals.	1	2	3	4	5
16.	I have assessed where I am currently relative to the goals I want to achieve.	1	2	3	4	5
17.	I can clearly envision the ideal me.	1	2	3	4	5
18.	I can clearly envision the extraordinary life I want to create for the next five years.	1	2	3	4	5
19.	I have identified the obstacles to achieving my goals and identified solutions to those obstacles.	1	2	3	4	5
20.	I have an action plan for my most important goals.	1	2	3	4	5
		Total				

Finished! Have a cookie.

The Journey Together
Preparing for the Journey

The inner game — how you think and feel, and the messages you tell yourself — have an incredible impact on your success. We will talk more about that later. For now, let's identify your past successes and what you are most proud of. Pack these for the journey in a spot where you can review them often. Your journal is a good spot.

List past successes.
What are you most proud of?
Who are the people who will support you on your journey? List your team members.*
What other resources will help you on your journey? (strengths, energy, commitment...)

* I will introduce some people who have been on this journey and they will be with you in spirit.

Transformational Arc

Pack your bags; get ready for our journey! We will travel through six phases: Exploring, Building the Foundation, Clarifying, Embracing the Journey, Mastering Your Life, and Breaking Through to Success. Each phase will include tools and action steps to help you pursue your unique and extraordinary life.

Your journey will take you from where you are right now to a life beyond your wildest dreams! We will replace disempowering beliefs with vision that empowers and emboldens. This transformational arc describes six phases of the journey that you will revisit as you build mastery. Life is not linear, nor are these phases. The process is repetitive, your work in each phase builds on the prior phases. As you learn and grow, you will circle back to an earlier phase and apply learning in a deeper, more meaningful way.

The Journey Together
Exploring
Call forth your creativity and direct the inner critic to step aside. Explore your vision and dreams for the future. Surround yourself with people and things that inspire you. See all the possibilities and you will have an abundant supply of dreams. You deserve to dream. Imagine that you will succeed.

Building a Foundation
Build a strong foundation to support your dreams and vision to create a life that truly matters. This requires deep insight that comes with opening your heart and soul and listening to your intuition. With a clear sense of purpose and set of values, you will be able to establish priorities for the life you want. Your commitment will grow!

Clarifying
Focus on specific, worthwhile goals that are aligned with your vision, mission, and values. Focus your lens from long-term to today. You will learn and apply proven strategies that propel you to action and accomplishment. You see yourself already in possession of your goals. You realize increased self-esteem, confidence, and clarity.

Embracing the Journey
Break free of inner constraints. Let go of self-defeating habits and emotions that no longer serve you and make room to embrace all the good that is entering your life. You will grow in self-belief and will rely more on your intuition. Even the obstacles and difficult terrain will provide opportunities for growth. Experience deep emotional and spiritual healing. Unencumbered, you readily discover new dreams and a new ideal for your future self. You embrace the journey, yourself, and even life itself.

Mastering Your Life
Envision and move toward the ideal you! Commit to excellence! You are the artist creating your own life. Apply the same tools and process to other areas of your life: mental, physical, social, family, financial, professional, and spiritual. You have achieved extraordinary results in your life and have embraced empowering beliefs. You feel increased vitality, joy, and serenity. You are mastering life and living your greatness!

Breaking Through to Success
The world has been holding its breath, waiting for what only you can provide. You have broken through to success and have stepped into a new way of being; you are living a purposeful and meaningful life that only you can fulfill! You possess strong personal power, self-confidence, and self-esteem. You have created an extraordinary life. You set and realize new goals and visualize your extraordinary future while living deeply centered in the moment.

Let's get started!

Exploring

| Module 1 | Creating a Vision |
| Module 2 | Dream |

Building the Foundation

| Module 3 | Values, Mission, and Priorities |

Charting a Course

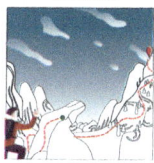

| Module 4 | Charting a Course |
| Module 5 | Achieving Your 90-day Goals |

Embracing the Journey

| Module 6 | Travel Light |
| Module 7 | Overcoming Obstacles |

Mastering Your Life

| Module 8 | Healing and Wellness |
| Module 9 | Enhancing Skills and Performance |

Breaking Through to Success

| Module 10 | Boldly Follow Your Dreams |

Module 1

Creating a Vision

> *"Whatever you vividly imagine, ardently desire, sincerely believe, and enthusiastically act upon, must inevitably come to pass."*
>
> — **Paul J. Meyer**

Objectives

At the end of this module, you will be able to:
- Identify the benefits of a vision
- Describe the power of guided imagery, or visualization
- Draft a vision of you 3 – 5 years in the future. Who will you be?

> *A vision is a bold, vivid picture in your mind fueled by emotion and all your five senses. A compelling, positive, personal vision describes the deepest yearning of your heart and draws you toward that future.*

Introduction

In the next two modules, we will explore your visions and dreams for your future. We will review the power of visioning, dreaming, and of guided imagery. I will share a couple of stories about people who have created and implemented a vision for their future and we will go on a couple of guided journeys into the future.

What is a vision, what are the benefits of having a vision, and how do you create one? A vision is a bold, vivid picture in your mind fueled by emotion and all your five senses. A compelling, positive, personal vision describes the deepest yearning of your heart and draws you toward that future. The paint is laid out before you; create your canvas of life. As you go through this session, the picture will become more detailed and more vibrant until, inevitably, it springs to life!

Celebration and Review

Congratulations on investing in yourself! You are going to be amazed! You have assessed where you are today, you have set three goals for the program, and packed your bags. We have reviewed the stages you will go through in the transformational arc, starting with Exploring. Let's examine the benefits of visioning, guided imagery, and visualization to explore possibilities for your future.

Benefits of a Vision

A vision improves performance, forms the basis of a plan, motivates you to excel, and provides focus and direction. Leaders, athletes, and successful people from all walks of life have realized the benefits of creating a vision. A vision serves as a beacon, beckoning one to a better future. It inspires and ignites enthusiasm. It enables you to see and attract opportunities that align with your goals.

Conrad Hilton imagined a string of hotels across the country when he was 12. Jean Claude Killy, the Olympic skier, saw himself winning three gold medals and became the first to realize this achievement. Research shows that leaders and organizations with vision outperform those without vision. Tom Watson, the founder of IBM, was once asked what he attributed the phenomenal success of his company to and he said it was three things. First, he created a very clear image in his mind of what he wanted his company to look like. Second, he asked himself how a company like that must act daily. Then, he put that into action.

Visualization of a positive future removes all mental blocks to success; it replaces doubt and worry with pictures of your success. The subconscious mind proceeds to do everything necessary to turn those pictures into reality. Visualization enables us to bypass that part of the brain that criticizes and judges; we tap into our unconscious, intuitive, fearless nature.

When we allow ourselves to take a magical trip to the future where anything is possible, we find meaning; we find the "why" for our lives. This enables us to have hope and diminishes anxiety and depression. We have a purpose.

Mahatma Gandhi envisioned India free from British colonialism and stated, "It is not the man who makes the vision; it's the vision that makes the man." Gandhi, he had a way with words.

How Do You Create a Vision?

Sometimes the vision grabs you. It is that incessant idea that begs for attention or the still small voice of wisdom within. Sometimes, an event might trigger your vision. During a middle school retreat, Kenneth dreamed of being a missionary in Mexico and went on to study Spanish and start an orphanage benefiting hundreds of children. Often when we are young, we have a dream of what we want our lives to become. As a child, my friend Liza dreamed of being a writer. She had her little desk and chair and made small booklets with stories. Through the power of guided imagery, Liza remembered these dreams. She went on to publish three books and to inspire many.

A vision is a picture in your mind. Your vision of your future comes from your dreams when your mind is free from doubt or worry; driven by people, places, things, and events that inspire you. It is important to continually generate dreams for all areas of your life, including: mental and physical health, family, friends, finances, career, and spirituality. Identify who you want to become, where you want to go, and what interests and ideas you have for all areas of your life. After I lead you through a brief exercise in which you will be free to dream, you will write them down without thinking about whether they are possible. Simply put, do not judge your dreams. Anything is possible! What if you cannot come up with anything or the idea of a vision is overwhelming? Just make something up! An ideal personal vision is vivid, specific, challenging, and is as far as you can see into the distant future.

My first time creating a vision occurred on a beautiful day with the one I loved. I sat with my future husband Bill on the dock at my grandparents' lakeside home on a glorious summer day. It was one of those days when anything seemed possible and we shared our dreams. I would be a consultant to businesses and help women to improve their lives; he would stay home with our beautiful, smart children. At 23, Bill was the Renaissance man: a fabulous cook, knowledgeable about politics, history, culture, arts, and science; a great sense of humor with a winning, outgoing personality. He makes everyone he meets feel comfortable and like themselves better. We would buy an old house and fix it up—notwithstanding that we didn't even own a hammer, much less know the difference between sheetrock and joint compound. We would travel the world and all who entered our home would feel the love and joy. Bill had recently graduated with a degree in Asian Studies and Anthropology and I would graduate with a bachelor's in Social Welfare as soon as I finished a single gym credit. Bill was in the restaurant business and I was doing direct care with developmentally disabled adults in community residences. Little did we know that all this and more would come to pass.

One of the tools we will be using throughout our journey together is guided imagery, a form of meditation and a proven method for tapping into your subconscious where judgment and self-limiting thoughts are bypassed. In a guided imagery, you will be asked to close your eyes and will be led through imagining a specific situation. There will be pauses to give you an opportunity to further create the scene. Since you are in a relaxed state, your subconscious is activated, and creativity is released.

The subconscious expresses itself through pictures. Guided imagery is a powerful tool. If you are reading this book, you can either have a friend read the guided imagery to you or you can read then close your eyes and experience the scene as described. You can also go to my website and listen to the audio version (background music from https://SilencioMusic.co.uk) wherever you see this icon:

The Power of Guided Imagery and Visualization

Guided imagery and visualization have been used by many in an infinite variety of ways. Athletes, leaders, healers, and therapists have all demonstrated the power of visualization. In guided imagery, someone else leads you through a script. In visualization, you envision the scenes yourself.

Mind

You have probably experienced visualization when loading your car with suitcases. Before picking up the heavy suitcases, you might imagine how they will best fit in your trunk. Or when you need a decision, you might play out different scenarios in your head before selecting the best option. When planning a trip, you might envision different routes and plan accordingly. Many people will practice giving a speech or an important sales presentation by mentally rehearsing. When thinking about something that occurred in the past, we typically see a picture in our mind. If it was a negative experience, we might replay that scenario over and over again making ourselves feel worse and worse. A positive memory can bring joy and when we picture something positive in the future, it can give us hope and anticipation.

Extensive research in the field of education demonstrates that visualization improves memory and learning. In the book, Super-Learning 2000,[1] Sheila Ostrander and Lynn Schroeder discuss numerous research studies that demonstrate how memory and test scores can be enhanced through visualization. Suggestive-accelerative learning and teaching developed by George Lozanov uses subconscious mental activity including positive suggestions, music, imagery, and relaxation to improve memory and learn new information.

Accelerated learning focuses on the whole person and uses guided imagery to improve memory and retention. The more vivid and ridiculous the images are, the easier they are to remember.

Sports Performance

Sports psychologist Richard Suinn, Ph.D., the first psychologist to serve on a U.S. Olympic sports medicine team in 1972 used a combination of imagery training, relaxation, and thought stopping during competitions. While practicing visualizing skiing, some of the athletes claimed they were cold. Suinn hooked up instruments to test the reaction of the muscle and found that the muscles when visualizing the ski run behaved the same way as when physically skiing and he theorized that the brain doesn't know the difference between actual performance and mental practice.

Since then, numerous studies have concluded that mental practice improves performance. Professional golfer Anika Sorenstam has said that visualization is her 15th club—she always imagines the perfect shot.[2]

Most elite athletes and many recreational athletes practice using guided imagery and visualization. Guided imagery has been proven to work in all sports. The more the athlete practices mentally, the better the results.

Wellness

Numerous studies demonstrate that guided imagery reduces stress, decreases pain, improves sleep and quality of life, decreases heart rate, and decreases respiratory rate in numerous disorders including immune system disorders, endometriosis, lupus, multiple sclerosis, and cancer. Guided imagery lowers cortisol levels, your body's main stress hormone known for the "fight, flight, and freeze syndrome," and increases your immune antibodies. Oncologists Bernie Siegel, M.D. and Carl Simonton, M.D. have been treating cancer patients using guided imagery with outstanding results since the 1980's. Guided imagery allows the patient to relax and envision healing; it helps the patient communicate with the disease and imagine cancer cells evaporating, and the patient's immune system follows suit.

Spirituality

A hopeless drunk looks forward to a visit from an old drinking buddy; drinking and reminiscing about old times. He notices at once that his drinking buddy has changed considerably and that a miracle has taken place. The buddy declares that "God has done for him what he could not do for himself" and it is obvious that this man is now enjoying a life he had never known. Soon after, the drunk enters the hospital, as he had countless times before to help him recover from alcohol. Suddenly, he has a deep spiritual experience. He realizes that he must turn from self-centeredness to "the Father of light in all things." Once he accepts this, he immediately feels serenity. He has a vision of "thousands of hopeless alcoholics who might be glad to have what has been given so freely to me. Perhaps I could help some of them. They in turn might work with others."[3] Bill Wilson goes on to help Dr. Bob recover from alcoholism and together they found Alcoholics Anonymous. A.A. works exactly as Bill Wilson envisioned: one alcoholic helps another. Today, A.A. is found in more than 180 countries around the world with an estimated 2 million members.

Emotional/ Mental Health

Visualization is used in counseling to desensitize phobias, addiction recovery, weight control, improved relationships, and career and life planning. Guided imagery is used to enhance cognitive, emotional, and behavioral change. It is used in emotion regulation by recalling a past positive event. In therapy, mental imagery is used in rescripting past events into something more positive.

Module 1 — Creating a Vision

Leadership

Leaders are people with vision. Visualization is used to determine opportunities and alternative scenarios for the future. A clear vision of the future inspires followers, earning their commitment on a spiritual and emotional level. People become willing to overcome obstacles and endure hardships if they have a reason and an inspiring "why."[4]

Throughout this book, I will share some stories of people who have applied these principles. After each story, I will ask you a few questions to help you reflect on what you have read.

Story — Kenneth

Introduction to Kenneth

I have had the privilege of interviewing many leaders who have created and implemented a vision for success. I met Kenneth when I attended a convention for Leadership Management Incorporated, a firm that I represented as a distributor.

Kenneth

At the 1985 Leadership Management Inc. International Convention in Dallas, Texas, Kenneth, a tall, average-looking man in a brown suit, was introduced to give the benediction. As soon as he uttered the first few phrases of prayer, everyone knew that this was no ordinary man. As he prayed, he spoke with authority and a light seemed to shine forth. Later, as I was talking with my husband, who do you think was the first person who welcomed us to the convention? Kenneth. Little did I know that Kenneth was to become my sales manager for almost 10 years and that he would have a huge impact on my life. I have learned a lot from Kenneth; I have learned from his words and actions, but I think more importantly from the kind of person he is. Let me tell you a bit about his story.

When many of us were young, we had a dream; a dream of what we wanted to become. For some, the ideas emerge step by step. In others, the dream occurs in a sudden awareness, a gift from God presented as a picture, stirring the spirit, and awakening the soul.

Kenneth grew up in Missouri, where diversity meant that there was talk of one Hispanic family out of thousands of white families, but no one actually knew them. In middle school, Kenneth attended a men's retreat where he met people from around the world, including several people from Mexico. Mexico intrigued him. Suddenly, an exciting idea took hold of him mentally, physically, and spiritually. With abrupt clarity, he saw himself establishing churches in remote areas of Mexico. He saw himself as a bush pilot, flying a plane to get to these areas. Although he was still sitting in the retreat, it seemed that someone had switched the channel and he was a missionary in Mexico. The vision came fast, yet the path emerged slowly with each step.

His vision to become a missionary in Mexico influenced many decisions, including the classes he took in high school, the college he attended, and the woman he would marry. Beginning in high school, Kenneth studied Spanish. He found one of the few Hispanic families in Missouri and practiced speaking with them. He chose a Christian college with a missionary program. When Kenneth met Wanda, the woman who would later become his wife, he told her that he wanted to be a missionary in Mexico, and when she enthusiastically gave her support, they married. After marriage and the birth of their first son, Kenneth and Wanda welcomed foster children into their home.

Kenneth says his faith in God and belief that his vision could be accomplished grew each time he developed a more detailed plan of action. Each new step uncovered obstacles and roadblocks along the way. He learned that he needed more than his personal belief; he needed support and help from others. He needed the support of his wife and family, he needed the support of other missionaries, he needed money to finance the mission, and he needed the support of the government in Mexico. He needed to engage others in his dream! Kenneth went to Mexico to assess the needs and to decide how he could best serve as a missionary. Missionaries he spoke to described the needs of families too poor to care for all their children and who found it necessary to drop one or more children off at an orphanage or church. They described orphaned children living on the streets. They suggested to Kenneth that, since he had experience with foster children and adoptions, he would be able to meet this need in Mexico. He saw the need firsthand, took many photos, and developed a plan to open an orphanage in southern Mexico. With the photos and detailed plan, Kenneth painted a compelling story that inspired his wife and people in his church to support the mission.

Kenneth's church in Missouri agreed to provide the initial funding. With some funding assured, Kenneth moved his family to the Mexico City area and began taking in children. He called the orphanage "Niños de México AC," which means "Children of Mexico." The concept was to group the children and care for them as a family unit. He built a home with a square courtyard in the middle. Again, he used photos to obtain the financial support the orphanage required. Over the course of 12 years, Niños de Mexico grew to 100 children and is still that way today. He had a budget of

$250,000 per year. 85% of the income came from churches in Missouri.

Fortunately, Kenneth never succumbed to the thought that his dream was unattainable. He didn't always know how it could all be accomplished but could always determine the next step. Each step brought his vision into sharper focus and enabled Kenneth to positively impact hundreds of children who walked through the doors of Niños de México.

Kenneth told me, "it is easy to be stymied or feel held back by problems in the moment. Create a written dream list and a plan of action. Then take a step and welcome the obstacles because they will expose the problems that lead to your next steps. Take action and, eventually, your dream will come true."

Discussion

How did you feel about this story? What resonated with you? What did you learn about how this person created and implemented his vision? What could you apply?

Feelings	Thoughts that resonated with you — Did you have a dream in middle school?
Action you will take	

Guided Imagery — The Path

Introduction to "The Path" Guided Imagery

You can expect one or two guided imageries in each module. Typically, I begin a guided imagery meditation with a script designed to help you relax. Here, we will follow a progressive relaxation exercise to relax your body and open your mind to free you from fear, doubt, and worry and promote your best dreaming. You could have someone read this to you or you could read it and then follow the instructions. The further into the future that you envision, the greater the possibility; you don't need to be practical. I will ask you to pick a period of time three, five, or ten years in the future. Choose the furthest distance in time you can see.

The Path

Lie down with your legs uncrossed and your arms at your sides. Let your eyes close. Take a slow, deep breath, expanding your chest and abdomen. Pause a moment, then exhale slowly, feeling your chest and abdomen relax. Breathe in this way until you begin to feel quite relaxed. As you become more relaxed, your breathing will become slow and even. You now feel calm and comfortable.

Feel your feet and legs. Imagine them becoming very heavy. Say to yourself, "my feet are relaxing, they are becoming more and more relaxed ... My feet are deeply relaxed." Feel your ankles, lower legs, and thighs. Imagine them becoming very heavy. Say to yourself, "my ankles, lower legs and thighs are becoming more and more relaxed. They are deeply relaxed." In the same way, relax your stomach, chest, back... Say to yourself, "I am becoming more and more relaxed ..." Relax your hands, forearms, upper arms, and shoulders. Feel them becoming very heavy. Relax the muscles of your neck and jaw, allowing your jaw to drop. Relax your face, your tongue, eyes, and forehead. Enjoy the feeling of total body relaxation. You are now in a calm, relaxed state of being.

You are about to begin a journey ... A journey where you are free to be you ... You set the pace ... You are walking along a path in a beautiful green meadow. It is a wonderful sunny day. Feel the warmth on your face. Notice the rich yellow color of the sun and imagine the yellow warmth soaking into your skin ... Let the warmth soak deeply into your skin ... Let the sun heal you ... Let the warm yellow energy fill your lungs and extend into every organ of your body and every cell ... through your legs to your toes ... your arms to your fingertips ... If you have any cares or worries, let them go ... You won't need them on this journey ... Everything you need is being provided ...

A warm, gentle breeze refreshes you. Breathe in peace ... breathe out all concerns ...

You see all types of flowers. Smell the fragrance. Perhaps you see daisies, tulips, lilacs, lavender ... Look around and appreciate this ... You have this all to yourself ... Gentle rolling hills ... calm ... relaxed ... Breathe ... Notice a tree growing up towards the sky ... You can see from the thickness of the trunk that this tree has been here for a very long time ... notice branches that reach out with joy ... The green leaves open to the nourishment of the sun... the roots extend deeply ... receiving nourishment ... sending the energy throughout every branch to every leaf. Imagine for a moment that you are like the tree ... with your feet on the ground, receive the energy from the earth, nourishing and strengthening you ... grounding you ... empowering you ... imagine your arms outstretched to embrace it all ... let your heart open to the warmth of the sun ...

feel the spirit that belongs to everyone ... this higher power... experience that which is all-knowing, all-loving, and all-wise ... you are all-knowing, all-loving, all-wise...

You come to a river ... Notice how the water flows ... Perhaps it flows gently ... Maybe rapidly ... whatever you experience is okay ... Spend some moments watching ... Let go of anything you no longer need and allow it to be carried away by the water ... a past hurt ... a resentment ... fear ... you won't need those here ... In the distance, you see a beautiful bridge. See the colors and design of the bridge as you approach more closely ... This bridge is your bridge... This is a magical bridge ... It will take you to the magical place where anything is possible... Walk towards the bridge.

As you step on the bridge you feel the magic of the place ... the bridge will carry you to the future ... 3 or 5 or 10 years into the future ... You select the time... whatever comes into your mind ... go further into the dream state ... where anything is possible ... where you feel whole ... the bridge may be short or long ... you cross ... as you reach the land, notice that someone is there waiting for you... a person... a spirit... you are given something you have longed for ... an image ... an object ... a scene ... a thought ... whatever you imagine is right for you ... take some moments to enjoy it ... you have prepared these past years for your life's work ... it is what you were meant to do ... your gift to the world ... take some moments to allow yourself to fully enjoy it ... your labor of love has brought much fruit ... enjoy the fruits of your labor... the people in your life... the quality of your relationships ... The things you have done together over the years ... your health and fitness ... the things you have learned ... your connection to your higher power... your contributions to others ... your financial health and some of the ways you have enjoyed your earnings ... travel ... stuff ... Now, imagine your perfect day from the time you get up ... your home ... your loved ones ... your time together... your passion ... take some moments to fully enjoy your life ... Look back over the past years and note some of the key events, signposts along the way ... a key step or steps you took ... You can return to this magical place whenever you like ... It is time to cross the bridge from the magical to this moment ... cross the bridge ... see a flight of steps and take the first 2 steps with each step feel more and more alert ... steps 3, 4, 5 you feel your fingers and toes. 6, 7 hear my voice and the sounds around you ... 8, 9 feel the chair 10 when you are ready, gently and gradually open your eyes ...

Guided Imagery Reflections

In your notebook jot down a vision for your future in three, five, or ten years. Through the course of this journey you will have the opportunity to clarify and build on this vision. It does not need to be perfect! Did anything surprise you? How did you feel about yourself? Did you feel your strength and power?

An example — My 5-year vision written when I was 28 years old

I am 33 years old. I have a wonderful relationship with Bill and our two children. We are making $120,000 per year. I earn $50,000 per year. I am very active in the spiritual community and socialize with these people. Bill and I take many vacations and have been to Europe and many other amazing places.

I have a strong faith in God which gives me an inner peace. I am still aggressive in seeking business and the things I want in my personal life. However, I am far more consistent and act out of love rather than anger and fear. Although I am a loving, concerned person, I am also a realistic businesswoman. I know where I am going and how I am going to get there. I do not let other people interfere with my dream machine and my goals. I am confident rather than cocky. I truly see the humor in life and enjoy it to the fullest. I am not sarcastic or flippant. I am goal oriented, yet I live one day at a time.

I run 5 miles daily, ran a marathon, and am in excellent health. I feel light and thin and full of zest. I have a positive mental attitude.

> *"Whatever you can do, or dream you can, begin it. Boldness has genius, power, and magic in it."*
>
> *— Goethe*

(Goethe was an artist, critic, novelist, poet, scientist, playwright, statesman, and theatre director, and lived a bold life)

Module 1 — Creating a Vision

Three – Five – Ten Year Vision

Draft a word picture of your desired future. Write today's date and the future date.

Reviewing Your Vision

Is your vision inspiring and compelling? Does it describe what you truly want for yourself? Sometimes, we get caught up in what others want for us or what the media tells us is important. We are steeped in a culture that tells us that it is important to be thin, young, and wealthy. It tells us that it is important to consume and to create an image on social media that shows an idealized version of ourselves. It is time for a shift in thinking from the world's ideals to God's ideal for us. Is it loving or is it ego? In recovery, we ask "does it bring me closer to a drink or closer to sobriety?" Include the deepest longings of your heart, the feelings you want to have and how others respond to you and your success. Listen to your intuition.

Desired Future State versus Current State

I don't shop like other people. When I go to a shopping mall, I usually have one store in mind and I want to get in and out of there as quickly as possible. I go to the map and find the store. But I can't get to my destination until I find the "you are here." Once I know where I am and where I want to go, I can create a path forward. To reach your vision, it is important to know where you are currently.

Describe or draw important features of your desired future state. Then describe or draw the same features of your current state as honestly as you can without exaggerating. Here is my example.

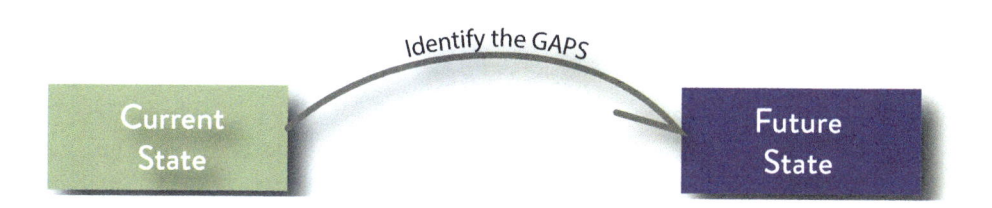

Current State → Identify the GAPS → **Future State**

Module 1 — Creating a Vision

Example of Desired Future State vs. Current State

Desired Future State Example	Current State Example
• A wonderful relationship with Bill and our two children.	• Good relationship with Bill but no children.
• Earn $50,000 per year.	• Lose $5,000 per year.
• Active in the spiritual community and socialize with these people.	• Just started in recovery.
• Bill and I have been to Europe	• Only travel in US and Canada.
• A strong faith in God which gives me an inner peace.	• A strong faith in God but no reliance on God or inner peace.
• Act out of love rather than anger and fear. I am a loving concerned person. I see the humor in life and enjoy it to the fullest.	• Resent everyone I know.
	• I am self-centered.
	• I take myself very seriously. I feel invisible.
• I live one day at a time.	• I am afraid. I don't want to be in my own skin. I just stopped drinking.
• I run 5 miles daily, ran a marathon and am in excellent health.	

The Difference Between Vision and Current State Example

- 2 children
- $55,000/ year
- Not part of recovery community
- Never been to Europe
- Lack inner peace
- Let other people influence how I feel
- Focused on self not others
- Live in the future and past, not present

Now you try!

Desired Future State	Current State

Good work! Now describe the difference between your desired results in life compared to your actual results. Don't try to figure out how to close the gap.

The Difference Between Your Vision and Current State:

Story — Liza

Introduction to Liza

Throughout this journey, I will share the stories of people who sat in my living room visualization groups and others I interviewed. I would like to introduce you to my friend Liza, a member of our first group.

Liza

As I think of Liza, I remember all the times we shared "a nice hot cup of tea" curled up in comfy chairs sharing what was going on in our lives, our hopes, our dreams, our challenges. Liza had many challenges and I admire her greatly. Born and raised in a small, mountain town, one of nine children, she had married, had a child, and divorced. She had been raising her daughter on her own for most of her daughter's life.

Liza moved to a larger city to complete her bachelor's degree and had been sober for a couple of years when we met. I was glad that Liza joined our visualization group. The group was a way for her to develop relationships and a support group with other women in the area.

The format was simple; I led the women through a relaxation exercise and then led them through a guided imagery of a scenario taking place in the future. Each woman shared what they experienced and described any new ideas and feelings that emerged. Liza envisioned the type of work she wanted to do and was surprised that part of what she envisioned was writing children's stories. In the past she had developed a prototype for a magazine for kids. Then, she remembered: she had always wanted to create children's books.

She shared; "When I was little, I had dreams for myself; I knew from a young age that I wanted to be a writer." Drinking erased those dreams, and she forgot her joy in making little books and reading all the time. The girl who bought a second-hand desk and created a writer's space decorated with a poster of a dog with a quill in its mouth was forgotten.

"When I started drinking, I didn't have any goals beyond what was going to happen on the weekend. My high school guidance counselor asked me why I wanted to go to college. For me, it was all about the parties. The guidance counselor suggested I go for journalism, but I didn't know what that was, and I didn't think I had the money.

"I enrolled at a community college in a program in journalism. Three days before classes started, my brother was diagnosed with a brain tumor and I was a mess for the first semester. At first, I got a lot of C's. I was used to getting A's. It was not a perfect fit; I was disappointed and constrained by the pyramid style of writing journalists employed; I wanted to be a fiction writer. Everyone else in my classes wanted to be Woodward and Bernstein or a sportswriter. One teacher gave me a lot of encouragement. I started working on a student newspaper and discovered working and writing is always easier within a group."

Liza graduated summa cum laude with a BA in English and a minor in journalism. Following her graduation from college, she immediately began working as a reporter for her hometown paper. One by one, each dream was exchanged for a drink. Her life began going downhill fast and she skidded to the bottom, her bottom. She'd had enough. Liza quit drinking and decided to work a program of recovery. Her life began to change for the better. At 28, she took a couple of classes in literature and loved it. With her daughter, now 8 years old, she moved to Albany and enrolled in the Graduate Program at the University at Albany to study literature.

The visualization group reintroduced Liza to the power of groups and the power of dreams—her dreams. Liza's life had been overwhelming, and she had gradually set all her dreams aside. She had no dreams and no goals. Initially, her dreams were like tiny seedlings and she quickly stepped on them before they could grow. One of the exercises that stood out for her was to focus on a goal with the perspective of having accomplished that goal, to picture it in detail with all the positive emotions related to that event. "Indelibly etched in my mind is the following (none of it true at the time)—I go into a bookstore and see my book on the shelf and am delighted and very satisfied. I feel healthy and enjoy a positive relationship with my daughter. Not wanting to block God I pray, 'This or something better.'" With the different types of visualizations, her awareness grew, and the possibilities expanded. She experienced a process of discovery; envisioning what she could become. Many things came true; some things did not come true or came in different forms. "My faith in God grew. Faith and sobriety were essential to realizing my dreams."

Liza learned how to set goals step by step. She set a goal to write a certain amount each week, kept a binder handy for writing, and reported back to the group. She was accountable to others for implementing her goals. Finally, she had enough written to submit her book to the Writer's Voice Competition. She envisioned winning the $1000 award and seeing her book on the shelf of the local bookstore. The judge at the event was Catherine Patterson, who wrote *Bridge to Terabithia*. Liza won the award and received very encouraging words from Patterson. Liza went on to publish her book, now available at bookstores across the country.

She continued her studies and earned a master's degree in English/Creative Writing. At this point, she was working for a teachers' union and had written a story about a

Module 1 — Creating a Vision

principal who had tackled a student gunman. She received a call from the Reader's Digest and thought someone was playing a joke on her. It was genuine, to her surprise, and she was later blessed with the opportunity to write the story for them. She has also written for Adirondack Life Magazine, Hudson Valley Magazine, and Yankee Homes. Her high school called and asked her to be the commencement speaker. Tears of gratitude ran down her cheeks as she recalled speaking at her high school.

Visualization helped to fuel lofty and exciting dreams. "As I envisioned going down the stairs in a beautiful old staircase, I became more and more relaxed, and my mind could wander without restriction, without judgment of what is possible or not possible. My wildest dream was to go to Paris, to immerse myself in the atmosphere inhabited by famous writers. On my fiftieth birthday, I ate at the Deux Magots, the café in the St. Germain des Prés neighborhood that had been frequented by Ernest Hemingway, James Joyce, Simone de Beauvoir, Jean-Paule Sartre, and Albert Camus. Each day I walked all over Paris, absorbing the culture, the food, the people, and the museums."

Now, when Liza goes into a bookstore, she sees her three Adirondack Adventure books in the middle school section. She has visited classrooms all over New York State and even visited the International School in Dusseldorf, Germany! She continues to participate in her writing group; she supports other authors by listening to them and reading and editing their work. She continues to share her work with a group and receives encouragement. She is energized by people who are growing and doing more with their lives. Liza energizes others and gives them hope and encouragement. She continues to nurture her dreams. She envisions a publisher for her new young adult book, making the book into a movie, and writing a daily meditation book. She envisions having the energy and resources to conduct research and promote her work.

Discussion

How did you feel about this story? What resonated with you? What did you learn about how this person created and implemented her vision? What could you apply?

Feelings	Thoughts that resonated with you

Action you will take

"Would you tell me please, which way I ought to go from here?"

"That depends a good deal on where you want to get to," said the cat.

"I don't care where," said Alice.

"Then it doesn't matter which way you go," said the cat.

— **Lewis Carroll**
Alice in Wonderland

What does the Research Say?

I have worked with individuals and organizations for the past 30 years to create and implement a compelling vision for the future. I have interviewed leaders and learned how they created and implemented a vision for their lives. Based on numerous case studies, many of which you will read in this book, I believe people who create a vision of their future and set written goals to achieve it realize an extraordinary future. And, alcoholics and other chemically dependent individuals stay clean and sober.

Most of the research on vision relates to leadership in an organizational setting rather than personal vision. Mark Lipton completed his doctoral dissertation on organizational visions of America's most successful organizations. In an article, he analyzed more than 30 international studies that focused on organizational vision and showed concrete, measurable, and meaningful performance improvement. He identified five benefits of an organizational vision, and I have translated that research to examine the benefits of personal vision.

Impact of Organizational Vision[5]	Impact of Personal Vision
1. Improves performance	Those with a challenging, vivid, and specific personal vision set challenging, vivid, and specific goals and accomplish them.[6]
2. Promotes change	Individuals change to align their behavior with their values.
3. Forms basis of strategic plan	Individuals committed to personal vision will develop more specific short-term goals and strategies to help them get there.
4. Motivates individuals	Individuals are motivated to reach their meaningful vision.
5. Provides focus and direction	Individuals will focus and sustain their effort to accomplish vision and goals.

These benefits apply to the individual as well. In addition, the use of guided imagery in career counseling and life planning has increased, enabling individuals to generate future scenarios and try on alternative choices.

My work experience tells me when you have a vision for your future and you frequently time travel to that desired future, your optimism and self-confidence grows.

Psychosocial research demonstrates that people tend to prefer a meaningful life as time increases into the future and prefer pleasure in the near future. In the long term, we focus on the "why," whereas in the short term we focus on the "how."[7]

In the short term, we tend to focus our goals to meet an immediate need. As we extend the time period to three, five, or ten years into the future, we express the desire for meaning in our life.

Action Steps

Directions: check each circle when completed:

1. Start a book for your personal strategic plan. Purchase a 3-ring binder and insert filler paper. I have a leather binder and have used it for over 40 years. I had to buy some of those reinforcement tabs. After all the page flipping; pages started trying to escape. ◯
2. Draft your personal and, compelling vision of your future in three, five, or ten years. ◯
3. Review the goals you set for this program. Analyze: Are your goals steps to achieve your vision? ◯
4. Clarify the results you want to accomplish during this program. ◯

Reflections

1. Start a new journal with a book that isn't digital or contains tear-out pages. Describe the benefits to you of having a clear and compelling vision for your future. ◯
2. What is the downside of not having a clear and compelling vision for your future? ◯
3. Reflect on how you feel about your draft vision for the future. ◯
4. Is it compelling, specific, and vivid? Does it energize you? What would help you feel better about it? ◯
5. List the people who will support and help you to accomplish your goals. ◯

Module 2

Dream

> *"The future belongs to those who believe in the beauty of their dreams."*
>
> — *Eleanor Roosevelt*

Objectives

At the end of this module, you will be able to:

- Develop a list of dreams in all areas of your life
- Create a vision board

Introduction

Your dreams are ideas for your future. Examine your vision and you will see that it is made up of numerous dreams. We started with the big picture and now explore additional ideas. During this module, you will explore all the possibilities for your future. As the chief creator of your life, you are always creating. I encourage you to look at the world with a new lens and identify fun, bold dreams! You will have the opportunity to look at all areas of your life and assess where you are on the wheel of life.

Celebration and Review

Congratulations! You have started creating your amazing life by drafting a personal vision. You have identified your past successes, what you are most proud of, and have listed the people whose support and help you need. You have identified where you are now relative to where you want to go. Both Kenneth and Liza described how important it was to engage people to support their goals. Life is easier and more fun when we are connected to others who love and support us.

Why Dream?

Your dreams are God's whispers to your soul. Pay attention! Listen and write them down. They are not commitments or goals, but they provide the colors and textures of your goals. The more dreams you have, the more choices you have about what is important to you. Dreams provide the energy to act and create your future. So, ignite your imagination and let it take flight. Write down all the dreams you have for your future—every place you want to go, who you want to become, what you want to learn, people to meet. Then, take those dreams and make them bigger, more colorful, more outlandish. Write down everything (**everything**) that makes your heart sing and energizes you. Dreams keep you motivated and interested in life. Without dreams, depression can set in. Continue to dream often and dream big. When you achieve your dreams, you will have other dreams to inspire you.

Best Practice Habits of Thought

Your beliefs and attitudes are habits of thoughts and these habits influence your actions. If you are afraid to look foolish or don't feel safe, you will hold back and not try. For some of us, coming up with dreams is a daunting exercise. Caroline couldn't come up with more than two dreams until she let her inner dreamer soar. Let's take a look at some common thought patterns that hold us back from dreaming — the fear of failure, the inner critic, external naysayers, and the scarcity mentality.

Fear of Failure

If you absolutely couldn't fail, what would you want your life to look like? What does your home look like, imagine the relationships you have with your family and friends, where would you live? What places would you travel to? What adventures would you have? What sport, exercise, dance, instrument, or music would you like to be better at? Do you have a book inside you? Describe the emotions you want to have on a regular basis, perhaps joy, peace, fun, happiness, love, compassion... Do you enjoy nature, cities, or both? What do you wish you knew more about? Think back to when you were younger, what dreams and interests did you have then? What does your dream job look like? What does the perfect retirement look like? Finding the perfect chocolate chip cookie is on my dream list.

The Inner Critic and the Naysayers — Silence This!

Most of us have the inner voice that tells us to be practical and that our ideas are not possible or are stupid. Societal norms influence us — girls aren't good at math and can't be engineers. It is not okay to speak up or to even take up space.

I tell my inner critic, "Thank you for the information, now go away!" While the inner critic tends to be loud and pushy, the small voice of intuition is gentle and patient. Listen to your intuition. The answer to what you can become lies within you. We have been conditioned to allow other people and circumstances to dictate who we are. Please yourself and live up to your own expectations. Wake up your power within! What would a positive review look like? What positive words would describe you?

Other may try to persuade you to stick to the tried and true, to not step out of bounds. They may try to discourage you, "for your own good"! The benefit of guided imagery and meditation is that you bypass the inner critic. And you can disregard the outer critics—tell them to live their dreams too!

The Scarcity Mentality — There is Enough To Go Around!

As a child, I was told to eat everything on my plate because children were starving in other countries. Despite the fact that my eating didn't help a child in a developing country, I ate everything on my plate. And, being one of six children, I ate really fast before a sibling finished something I wanted. After dinner, my mom proudly stated, "there isn't anything left, I made just the right amount!" We were still hungry. There wasn't enough and, furthermore, I didn't deserve it (was it because I didn't eat the peas?). In the past, maybe there was not enough or we were told there is not enough. For example, did you ever hear that money doesn't grow on trees? Examine whether this is true or an ingrained way of viewing the world.

Love grows when we share it; we don't use it up. Our share of love is infinite. When we share our ideas with others, they share theirs and our ideas expand. When we help someone else, we feel helped. When we achieve success or receive more money, others don't receive less. In fact, others become inspired by your success and we spend our money in ways that help others.

> *Your success does not depend on the failure of others.*
>
> *— Omar Suleiman*

Dreaming Big

You don't need to have a boring life or an ordinary life; you can have an extraordinary life! Every day is an opportunity to see the possibilities; extend your beliefs and dream bigger. In the *Course in Miracles* by Foundation for Inner Peace, published in 1976, there is no order of magnitude to miracles. A miracle is a change in perception. Take your dreams and dream bigger.

Most of the people I interviewed mentioned that they love to read biographies. They are inspired by the dreams and accomplishments of others and learn how others overcame obstacles. If someone else can do it, why not me? Read inspirational stories and listen to inspirational music. Identify people you admire and list the qualities you want to emulate and the lifestyle or career you want for yourself.

Watch Susan Boyle in her YouTube video from Britain's Got Talent and hear her sing "*I Dreamed a Dream*" from the Broadway show Les Miserables. She introduces herself as a 47-year-old woman from Scotland who lives with her cat Pebbles. Her dream is to be a professional singer and perform in front of a really large audience. A pan of the audience shows a few eye rolls. Susan Boyle opens her mouth and is amazing! Susan's audition in 2009 was the most watched YouTube video ever at that time with over 680 million views. She has sold over 120 million platinum and gold albums in 38 countries.[8]

My friend Beth told me about the beautiful brick stately home where she grew up in Albany, New York. Here is an example of dreaming big. When her dad was a boy, he delivered newspapers to that house. He loved the house; he could see himself living in the house and having a family there. One day, he was bold enough to ring the doorbell and he told the man who owned the house that he would like to live there. Twenty years later, the man bequeathed the house to Beth's father. Dreams are not limited!

Sometimes, someone else steps in and offers a dream that inspires us, and we say "yes, I want that too." My husband Bill was working as a waiter in a fine restaurant when another waiter who was 15 years older tapped him on the shoulder and said "Son, I'm going to make you a millionaire." He taught Bill how to save his money and how to invest it until he had enough for the down payment on a multifamily house. We drove by the house and we both said, yes, that is the one! Bit by bit, Bill renovated that house until the value tripled. In the meantime, one unit paid our mortgage, another unit paid the taxes, and the third unit paid our utilities. We lived for free and were on our way to financial security.

Module 2 — Dream

Dream Continuously

Dream continuously while living in the day and accepting where you are now. While reading magazines, note what draws your interest. It might be a story, a picture, or even an advertisement. I love travel magazines because they inspire me to visit new places.

I love to see beauty in nature, the arts, and music. My husband and I have been visiting the National Parks and photographing the amazing sites. We love the beauty and the diversity in cities: the little hole-in-the-wall cafés, the architecture, the museums, the different music venues. We do things that we had dreamed and we smile.

My friend Brandi, who lives on the East coast, dreamed of taking big, bold action in her career and in her life. While visiting California on vacation, the idea popped into her head to visit a business that had tried to recruit her years before. Within days, she accepted a fantastic job and signed a lease for a beautiful apartment. She came back to the East Coast, sold all her belongings, and started a bold, new life!

Identify what inspires you. If you could go anywhere and do anything, what would it be? Write it down. If you don't like your current situation, think about what you want instead. Paint a different picture. Be open to possibilities.

I am going to ...

"*If you can dream it, you can do it.*"

— **Walt Disney**

Story — Denise and Jason

Introduction to Denise and Jason

My most memorable New Year's Eve was spent with my husband, baby Sarah, and two other couples at Denise and Jason's home on the eastern tip of Long Island. Their home was filled with love and joy, and the most enticing smells and delicious foods came from Denise's kitchen. They proved that quality of life is far more important than money or prestige.

Denise and Jason

Denise and Jason both worked at the New York Stock Exchange on the floor as traders, a hectic, noisy, stressful job. They were very successful, and Jason was close to being offered his long-awaited seat in the Exchange. One evening, standing on the train home, Jason was unable to release his grip from the pole as he reached his stop. Jason was a nuclear submarine veteran, very comfortable with stress. Jason realized his body was telling him something.

On the weekend, Jason was restoring his Porsche and needed a part, which seemed to be available at a shop way out at the tip of eastern Long Island. Together, they drove to the shop and bought the part. Jason exclaimed to Denise that he would love to work in this premier auto restoration business and Denise replied, "So, why not do it?" Society says that a career in the New York Stock Exchange is filled with prestige and that is what we should desire. Jason wanted a stress-free job, time with Denise, and time to play golf. They went in to quit the next day and Jason was offered the seat on the exchange. They traded that opportunity for a new life in Eastern Long Island, with Jason repairing cars and Denise doing something she dreamed about, cooking at a restaurant. Although amazingly happy with their new lifestyle, they later traded these jobs. Dreams can constantly evolve, and it isn't until we try something that we know whether it is for us. Jason works for a golf course, and, before she retired, Denise worked for the tennis club. They have a full and rich life filled with nature, friends, travel and laughter. They are living the life of their dreams.,

Module 2 — Dream

An Example — A Portion of My Dream List written in December 1982, Age 26

- A wonderful relationship with Bill
- A good sense of humor
- Weigh 124 lbs.
- Great public speaker
- Professional trainer
- Lead growth groups
- Travel to Europe with Bill
- Write books
- Run 5–10 miles a day
- Happy children
- Spiritual
- Positive role model for women
- Great gourmet cook
- Interesting, warm, fun friends
- Warm supportive and loving
- Earn $100,000 per year
- Help others to grow
- Run a marathon
- Earn a master's degree
- Have a baby
- Stop drinking
- Visit China, Japan, Europe including Ireland, Italy, Spain, Paris, London
- Be a millionaire
- Have a Golden Retriever and teach him tricks

My Current State in 1982

Some of these dreams seemed achievable, others daunting. At the time, I was making $11,000 a year as a social work case manager in a nonprofit. I was teaching some workshops and led a group of developmentally disabled adults to set goals and get ready to move into their own apartments. I was far from being a professional trainer. I didn't know what that would look like. I had been drinking every day for the past eight years. I ran three miles most days, sometimes falling because I was still drunk from the night before. I couldn't imagine running a marathon. I was the kind of student who skipped gym and wasn't good at any sport. Travel to Europe? I didn't have a passport and it seemed very difficult and scary! Forget about having a baby! I couldn't take care of a pet.

My Future Dream List

Write down everything you've ever wanted, everything you would like to become or achieve. Allow your imagination to go wild. Add to this list on a regular basis. Date it, check it off when it becomes a goal, and highlight it when you have accomplished it.

My Dreams

Guided Imagery — Journey into the Future

Introduction to Guided Imagery

The beginning of this guided meditation will relax you. Imagine you are in an elevator and count backwards from 10, instructing yourself to become more and more relaxed with each passing floor until you exit at the first floor. We will immediately follow this with the guided imagery to help you envision your future in 3-5-10 years. Often, it is easier to visualize something longer term because our inner critic is fooled into allowing us to achieve more if we give ourselves more time. Sometimes you have to play mind games with your own mind. You could have someone read this to you or you could read it and then follow the instructions.

Journey Into the Future

We are about to embark on a journey, a journey into the future …

Before we begin, take off your judge's robe. Suspend disbelief. Suspend perception of time... You have permission to visualize whatever you can conceive of. Anything is possible. You can use this magic wand if you like.

Let's go to a very special place, a place where you are safe and free to dream, free to be yourself. This magic elevator will transport you there. As you enter the elevator, you realize that you are on the tenth floor. 9th floor, 8th floor, with every passing floor, feel yourself becoming more and more relaxed. 7th floor, 6th, 5th. More comfortable, a deeper stillness within you. 4th, 3rd any outside sounds only help you to become more relaxed. Relaxed yet very aware, you are in charge. If, for any reason, you don't like one of my suggestions, ignore it and replace it with something even better for you. 2nd, 1st floor.

The door opens and you step into your space. In front of you is a huge screen. Seat yourself at the beautiful, old desk facing the screen. On the left side of the desk is a globe—spin it... you are free to travel anywhere. It is as easy as putting your finger on anyplace on the globe. Telephone—you can contact anyone in the world, computer—you have access to all knowledge and access to people and the resources you need.

Now lean back and relax. Turn your attention to the screen.

The lights dim and a movie representing your future at any time period you choose begins on the screen. Whatever you choose will be right for you, 3–5 or 10 years into the future. Simply say the number to yourself.

Now, as though by magic you are no longer the observer, you are in the future. Imagine stepping into the movie and you are in the year ----. You are just waking up and you see light streaming through your window. It is a beautiful sunny day. You smell breakfast cooking and you think about the person or persons you are living with.

You have done many things together over the past years. Think about some of the enjoyable times you have spent together. See some of the things you did together. See your family... friends and colleagues ...and you are grateful for the warm, loving relationships you have had over the years. Take some moments and experience the positive relationships with others... See some of the things you have done... travel... recreation... community... cultural...

Realize that you have been able to enjoy life—your health is good. See yourself physically and emotionally healthy... energized and proud of how you look... After getting ready for the day and enjoying breakfast, you realize that you are dressed to go out and do your life's work. As you leave your home, look back and see where you are living. What kind of neighborhood, what does your home look like?

You are going off to do your life's work—it is what you have been preparing to do for many years... You feel fulfilled and creative... You arrive at the place where you do that work. You walk in and notice the wonderful atmosphere. Experience what that feels like... This place and the work you do fit you like a glove... Take a few moments and walk around, noticing how everything looks, the people, and the culture. And, today is your ideal day. Take a few moments to vividly see what you are doing... You know exactly what you are doing tonight. You are going to a banquet, an awards banquet. See all the people milling around. They are here, here to honor you... The emcee goes to the podium and asks that everyone take their seats. After a few moments, everyone is seated and a hush falls over the audience, a hush of expectation and pride. The emcee steps up to the microphone and begins describing the impact that you have had. Listen for a few moments as you are being introduced, listen to the impact you have had on others... Listen to the thunderous applause. You step up, and with deep gratitude, thank the people who have supported you along the way... You have and you are everything you ever wanted... You are who you are meant to be...

And now the dinner is over, it is time to go home and return to this room. Take a few moments and imagine that you are in the elevator once more. Floor 1, 2, 3, with every floor, you become more and more alert and ready to return to this room. 4, 5, 6, 7, feel the chair you are sitting on, 8, 9 hear my voice, 10; step out of the elevator and when you are ready, gently and gradually open your eyes.

Module 2 — Dream

Guided Imagery Reflections

Open your journal. Take a few moments to jot down a vision for your future in five years or ten years. What were the differences between what you envisioned in the previous guided imagery and this one? Did anything surprise you? How did you feel about yourself? Did you feel your strength and power? What happened at the banquet?

> *"Your boldest dreams are God's invitation to the greatest adventure of your life and they come to you because they are for you. Your dreams are placed in your soul as a pathway to releasing your potential and awakening your purpose for being."*
>
> *— July/Aug 2013 Daily Word by Kevin Kitrell Ross*

Story — Rhett

Introduction to Rhett

Rhett demonstrates that there is no limit to what you can dream and create. He surrounds himself with positive people and reads biographies of people who have achieved much. Plus, Rhett demonstrates faith in the power of what he envisions!

Rhett

Rhett had spent some time creating a dream list and, believe me, he had big dreams: to own a new van and boat, to travel to Israel, to be a guest on a national television show. At the time, Rhett was living in a budget apartment for $150 per month in upstate New York. I was impressed with Rhett's enthusiastic charisma and was surprised to learn that he suffered from depression and deep feelings of self-doubt. He wrote jingles for businesses' radio advertisements, such as the very successful local shopping mall jingle "Fashion is now! ... Fashion is now...."

He was part of a spiritual fellowship and wrote some Christian songs. On May 3rd, 1985, we both attended the Lincoln Law Banquet Christian Men's dinner with legendary attorney Sir Lionel Luckhoo, the featured speaker. Sir Lionel Luckhoo earned 245 consecutive murder acquittals and was listed in the World Book of Records as the world's most successful advocate. He was knighted twice by Queen Elizabeth, was the only person to serve as ambassador for two countries at the same time: Guyana and Barbados, and served as the Judge of the Supreme Court for Guyana.

During his speech, Sir Lionel Luckhoo passionately argued that the empty tomb is evidence for the resurrection of Jesus Christ and Rhett was so inspired that he wrote a song about the empty tomb. Rhett later shared the song with Sir Lionel and a friend, Dr. Mclaucklin.

The late Dr. McLaucklin asked Rhett to go to Israel to film his song, "The Empty Tomb." Dr. McLaucklin would pay for the video production; Rhett needed $3000 to fly to Israel, an amount he didn't have.

Rhett had helped encourage a man who was struggling through a divorce. The man subsequently asked Rhett to write a jingle for his business and paid Rhett $3000. It was the last day to buy tickets. "I'll never forget the feeling of waking up on the hill in Israel, and as the sun was rising, singing 'The Empty Tomb' at the location. At Sir Lionel's request, Pat Robertson invited Rhett to appear on his television program, the 700 Club. The video debuted on the 700 Club show and reached more people than Jesus had reached in his entire lifetime."

The next time I saw Rhett, he practically leapt across the room, overflowing with enthusiasm. He excitedly shared that he had just returned from Jerusalem where he was filmed singing his song, "The Empty Tomb," on location. At the time, I couldn't fathom how this opportunity had come about. According to Rhett, the only explanation for what happened was "providential intervention."

When I decided to write this book, I immediately thought of Rhett and this example of the power of visualization. I was delighted that my web search instantly directed me to Rhett's website, and I was not surprised that he had a radio show, had interviewed many politicians and celebrities, and was a motivational speaker. His website biography asserted that "Rhett Palmer is a man of many talents. He's an award-winning talk show host, singer/songwriter and 1st Place Vocalist in Nashville's Music City Festival, winner of two prestigious Gold Addy Awards, public speaker, and so devoted to his country he has been dubbed "Patriotic Palmer." I sent an email about the concept for the book and asked if I could interview him. Here is the response I received:

> Dear Linda!!!! Great to hear from you!!!! How did you find me???? Please stay in touch and I am moved that I am on your list! What a great idea for a book!!! You are a part of that success. Do you remember handing out yellow sheets to write down SMART goals? I wrote a few and then six months later a friend said "That is really something about that GOAL sheet" I replied "WHAT goal sheet???! Oh.... that goal sheet! mmmmm I took it out of my desk drawer there in Troy New York.... A new van...I now possessed it!!! A trip to Israel. I had just returned. From a visit on a national TV show. I had just been on the 700 Club!!!! A new boat...I had just taken possession of a new sea ray in exchange for advertising consultation. I could NOT afford a boat at that time in my life...last...a record released nationally...My new song at that time THE EMPTY TOMB was sent out to over 900 stations...the POWER of writing things down!!!!

I needed to find out if it was as easy as all that; what had helped Rhett to become the person he is? We scheduled a time to talk. Rhett told me his father died when he was young and he remembered becoming shy and withdrawn, spending his time reading biographies about the great people of this world. He read a book about George Washington Carver, which "planted

Module 2 — Dream

a seed of insatiable curiosity." He read Martin Luther King's books and biography and was "inspired by this brilliant man who left a profound legacy." Rhett was inspired to leave a legacy and traveled to Africa, Haiti, and Canada to serve with food distribution programs and mission work.

Faith has had a strong impact on Rhett's life. "Without faith, fear steps in and takes over. Faith makes belief possible." Rhett explained, "as a carpenter needs to believe that he will create a table or a house, a person with vision needs to believe that he will create the vision."

Sometimes hardships and obstacles lead to life changes that we could not have imagined earlier. In the early 90's, Rhett suffered from a breakup with his girlfriend. This devastated him so much that he left the advertising business and moved to Florida.

The Fourth of July 1993 marked a turning point in Rhett's career. He awoke that morning knowing that he had the opportunity to sing a patriotic song at the Dodgers baseball game. Rhett went to sleep that night with his own radio show. Fred, a Jewish man who had escaped the Nazis, appreciated Rhett's enthusiasm and asked whether he would like to have his own radio show. He took a boring show and grew it to The Florida Show, three hours of programming each weekday. Rhett found that through the power of the microphone, he could ask questions others were not allowed to ask. He met Mark Victor Hanson, Og Mandino, and Colin Powell. He has met with Kings and Queens, Zig Ziegler, Sir John Templeton, and Billy Graham. It wasn't always easy. Rhett was thrilled when he was able to set up an interview with Mike Wallace. It was cleared with the network and the program 60 Minutes. He flew to Martha's Vineyard to interview Mike Wallace, checked into a hotel, and was amazed when he received a room on the VIP level. He wasn't sure how he got that room. Gerald Ford was in the room next to him. When he arrived for the interview, he was told that it was canceled. He went into a deep depression and considered leaving Martha's Vineyard immediately. He stayed the weekend anyhow and went to the movies the next night. He noticed that Mike Wallace sat in front of him at the theater, introduced himself, and Mike Wallace invited him to a barbecue at his house the next day. Rhett got the interview!

I am not sure how I met Rhett—I think it was through our mutual friend David, who worked in my training business. They stopped at my house and together we dreamed dreams and talked about our goals for the future. I shared what I knew about the power of committing your dreams and goals to paper. They shared the power of committing your life to God. I remember Good Friday 1984; I was angry at God, but we were praying regardless. The thought to forgive God, as arrogant as that sounds, came to me. After some hesitation, I swallowed my pride and forgave Him, and begged for forgiveness in turn. A sense of peace surrounded me, and I was no longer angry. I understood that God had a plan and I was ready to accept it. It was a small step to, as we say in recovery, getting "right sized" with God. I remembered that there is a God and that I am not God. Within three months, I admitted I was powerless over alcohol and that my life had become unmanageable. I had dreams and goals but felt like an imposter helping others with goals when I wasn't making the kind of progress I wanted to make. I was far from the person who I knew I could be.

Discussion — Think for a minute and write.

How did you feel about this story? What resonated with you? What did you learn about how this person created and implemented his vision? What could you apply?

Feelings	Thoughts that resonated with you

Action you will take

Guided Imagery — The Beach

Introduction to Guided Imagery

This guided imagery is designed to relax and heal you.

The Beach

Get comfortable, relax, close your eyes, and imagine that you are on a quiet beach on a warm, sunny day. You are strolling along the beach. Feel the warm sand between your toes... feel the warm sun and a gentle breeze. Take in a deep breath and smell the fresh salty air. Become aware of the sun and let it heal every cell in your body and your mind. Let the golden light enter the top of your head and move throughout your body. See the sky and the clouds shapeshifting. Notice the rolling waves. Go to the water's edge and wade up to your ankles. Feel the cool water. Notice how the air feels on your skin. Hear the waves hitting the shore. Now imagine a chair appears in front of you... If you wish, there is an umbrella over your chair. Sit in the chair and watch the ocean. Notice the type of chair you are sitting in. See the sunlight dancing on the water, watch the waves rolling, and feel the peace of this moment.

Module 2 — Dream

Guided Imagery Reflections

Take a few moments to jot down any thoughts or feeling that occurred to you during this meditation. Did anything surprise you? How did you feel?

Balance Your Life

What does it mean to live a well-balanced life? Let's look at your wheel of life with each area that could be important to you. Imagine that the center of the below diagram represents 0 and the end of each spoke represents 100% achievement of your dreams in this area. Place a point along the continuum to represent where you stand now in that area. Connect the points. Is your life in balance?

What does life balance mean to you? Is it work-life balance or balance in all areas of your life, or is it balance in those areas most important to you in this period of time? There is no right or wrong here; define what is important to you. Identify which areas warrant the most focus. Balance your life and commit to rebalancing.

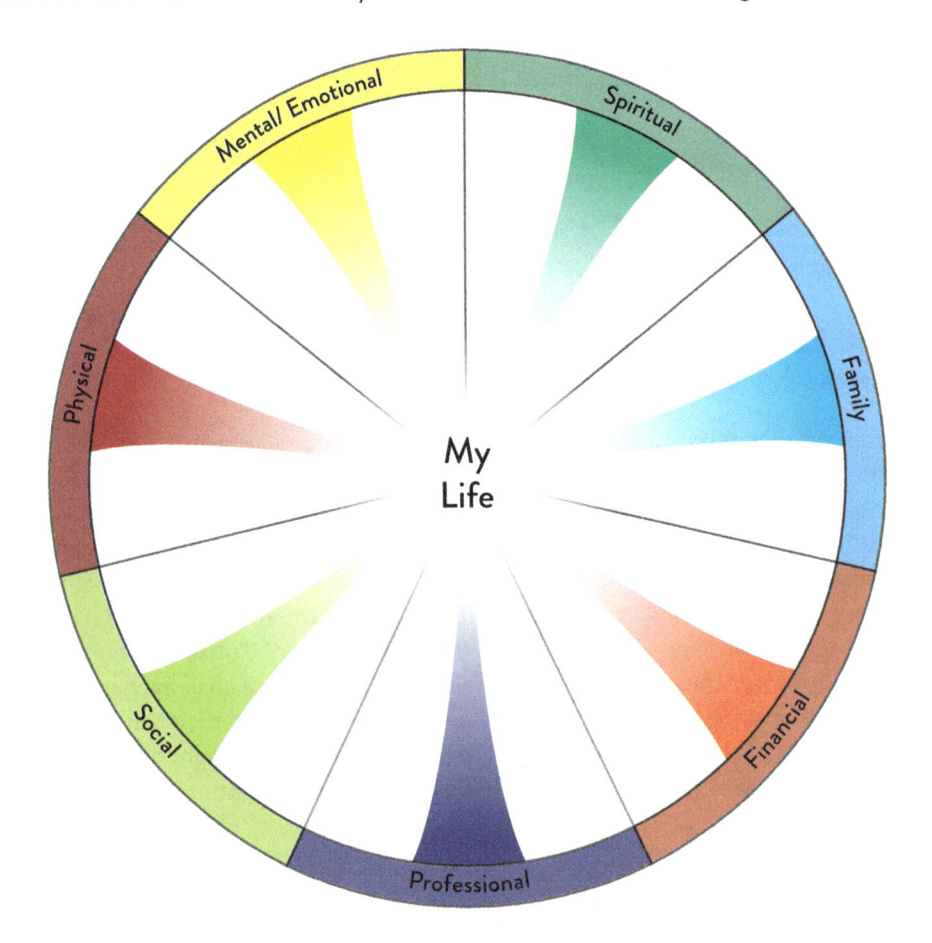

Wheel segments (clockwise from top):

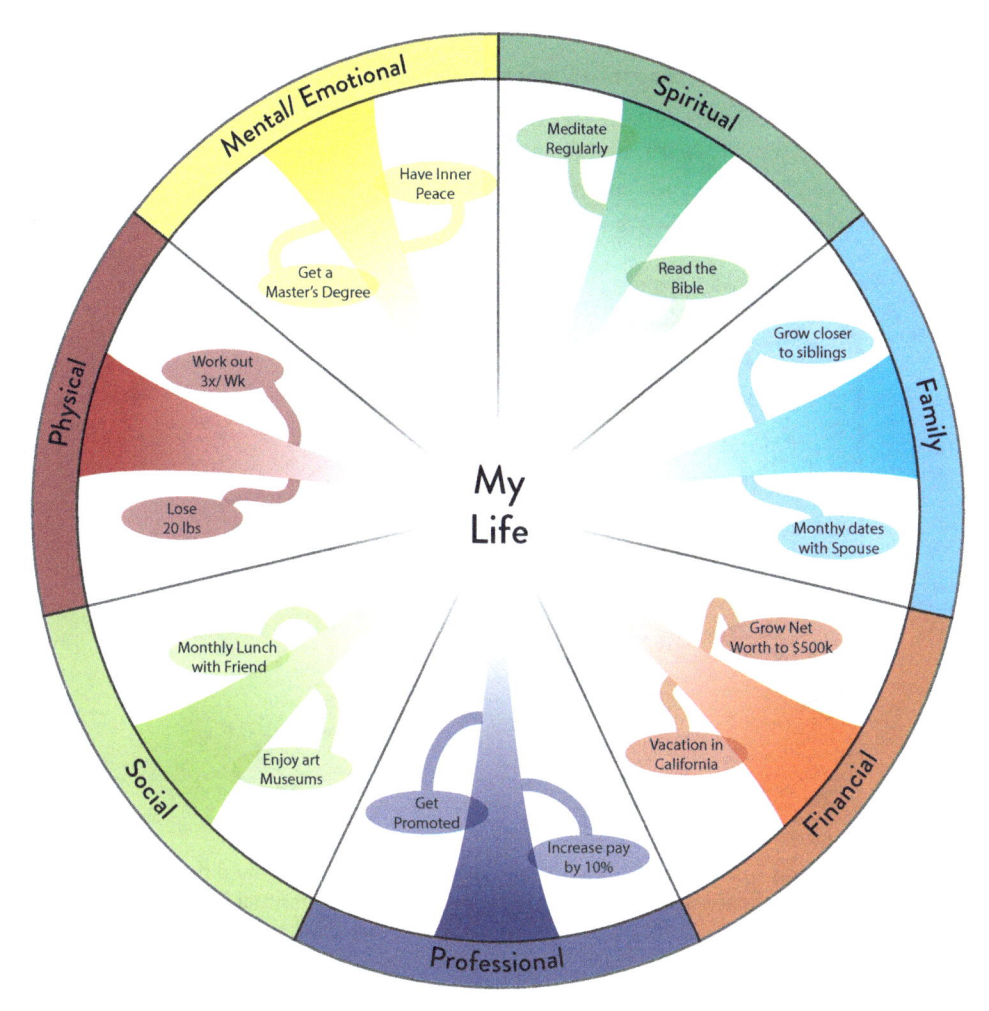

- **Spiritual**: Meditate Regularly; Read the Bible
- **Family**: Grow closer to siblings; Monthly dates with Spouse
- **Financial**: Grow Net Worth to $500k; Vacation in California
- **Professional**: Increase pay by 10%; Get Promoted
- **Social**: Enjoy art Museums; Monthly Lunch with Friend
- **Physical**: Lose 20 lbs; Work out 3x/Wk
- **Mental/Emotional**: Get a Master's Degree; Have Inner Peace

Center: **My Life**

Dreams for My Future

Identify your dreams for each area of your life and link them to the area in the diagram. Identify the areas most important to you.

Creating a Vision Board

A vision board is a collage of pictures that represent your preferred future life. The completed collage will inspire and focus you on your dreams. The pictures remind you of what is important and enable you to see yourself already in possession of the goal. It draws the future closer; the people and events needed for your desired future start to appear and your dreams are manifest. This works. Remember to celebrate the dreams that you realize and keep adding dreams.

Module 2 — Dream

How do I create a vision board?

Start with poster board, magazines, photos, scissors, and glue. Select pictures and words that represent who you want to become, how you want to feel, where you want to go, what you want to learn, etc. Arrange them as a collage and glue them onto the board. You can laminate your vision board to protect it. Put it in a place visible to you and know that these dreams are already in motion.

This is my vision board. Your vision board will look completely different. My vision board shows what is important to me: my spiritual life, love, loving my husband Bill, my mission, travel and friends all over the world, nature, beauty, fitness, joy.

Visualize it

Look at your vision board often. Put it in a place you see every day or plan to view it weekly over Sunday coffee. See it in your mind, making the experience as real as possible. See every detail. See it, hear what others are saying, smell the aroma of success! Let it gain substance. Experience the satisfaction of success! Give it energy. Now, make it a fact in the present! Act as if!

> "When I run after what I think I want, my days are a furnace of stress and anxiety; if I sit in my own place of patience, what I need flows to me, and without pain. From this I understand that what I want also wants me, is looking for me and attracting me. There is a great secret here for anyone who can grasp it."
>
> — Rumi, 13th century Persian poet

Story — Kate Pepin

Introduction to Kate

When I met Kate, she was a leader at a major university and, for her, work was a major source of frustration. Outside of work, Kate has shown a zest for life that I admired. By creating a collage of her future and envisioning that future, Kate has changed how she viewed the world and has been able to attract the kind of relationships and support that she needed. Rather than frustration, she has seen hope and has made progress with more soul-satisfying work.

Kate

Sometimes, it is just one small thing that will enrich our lives and give greater happiness. When we find our passion, our passion creates hope. I asked the participants in a workshop to create a collage to represent their vision for their future.

My friend Kate thumbed through magazines and noted a photo of a collaborative and fun work team. Kate's workplace lacked both personal enjoyment and teamwork. She took a chance and pasted the photo in her "Picture Your Future" collage. Her action nurtured her hope. Her hope impacted her vision; she started to see collaborative, fun people around her and began connecting with them. Kate was practicing positive expectancy. Kate now recognizes and attracts more positive and authentic people; not only did she find people at work that she can connect and collaborate with, but those connections led her to new experiences. She is more present and able to be in the moment with people. She accepts them where they are at and has learned building relationships increases the persuasiveness of data.

Kate has a personal mission to support the environment and nurture sustainability. She represented this on her vision board too. As a leader in facilities management at the university, Kate knew what she wanted to focus on but did not have the support of her managers. She was frustrated, and her frustration blocked her progress.

Soon after creating the vision board, the path to lead sustainability became clear. Kate was asked to represent her university in a regional business forum on sustainability. Through her new connections, she received recognition and support. Kate garnered funding from her university for a new sustainability initiative and collaborated with faculty members teaching sustainability to business students.

Kate integrated sustainability in her work by building with the lowest carbon footprint, using recycled materials and environmentally friendly HVAC systems, reducing energy consumption, and minimizing maintenance hours. She led projects with student involvement, including a high-density garden that supplies the student food bank, an important asset to the 47% of the students who are low-income. To gain support from leaders, Kate hosted a "50-mile meal" where all the food came from within 50 miles to demonstrate the energy impact of buying food locally.

Kate retired and has focused on making her own home more sustainable by adding solar panels, re-insulating the walls, updating the lighting with LED, and changing some windows to be more energy-efficient. She has an electric car and powers her long-range battery with solar power in the house at night when energy use is low. She grows much of her own food and buys the rest locally. Kate enjoys making art with recycled or forged materials. Kate was awarded a scholarship to assist her in her development as a mosaic artist. Kate will be studying with artists and sculptors in Tennessee and Michigan. Kate was awarded a scholarship to assist her in her development as a mosaic artist. Kate will be studying with artists and sculptors in Tennessee and Michigan. Kate now feels she is on the right path; her faith has been enhanced and her gratitude has grown. She realizes that many of her goals were just "to do" items and that what creates her emotional passion is encouraging sustainable action and collaborating with people who share her passion and positive attitude. By letting go of ego and the certainty that she was 100% right, Kate is now a collaborator who sees all that is good in the planet and every individual. Due to her work envisioning a better future and creating a vision board to represent that life, Kate has manifested a fun, collaborative, and environmentally sustainable life.

Lilly of the Wood

www. Katepepinarts.com

Discussion

How did you feel about this story? What resonated with you? What did you learn about how this person created and implemented her vision? What could you apply?

Feelings	Thoughts that resonated with you

Action you will take

What does the Research Say?

Guided imagery widens our perspective of future possibilities. Like trying on different outfits, we get to try on different roles and see how we feel. We can adjust the scenario and find something more fun, more powerful, or bold. Our options are unlimited. Using guided imagery is more powerful than the typical process of career planning that relies on vocational tests and feedback from the career counselor.[9] Guided imagery supports career and life decision-making, clarifies career identity and assumptions, and enables the individual to construct a story for their future congruent with their needs.[10]

When we create a vision board and consistently see it in our mind's eye, we are mentally rehearsing our future. Research shows that the more we mentally rehearse, the more our performance improves, the more optimistic we are about our future, and the more we believe that it will happen.

Module 2 — Dream

Action Steps

Directions: check each circle when completed:

1. If you absolutely couldn't fail, what would you want your life to look like? Generate a list of dreams for all areas of your life. ○
2. Identify people who have what you want — list them on your dream list. Learn about people who will inspire you to greatness by reading biographies and finding leaders you want to emulate. ○
3. Create a Vision Board and place it where you can see it daily. ○

Reflections

1. How did it feel to list your dreams? Was this easy or difficult for you? ○
2. Was there a time when you had more dreams, or it was easier for you to dream? ○
3. Journal on the process of creating your vision board and how you feel about the completed vision board. ○

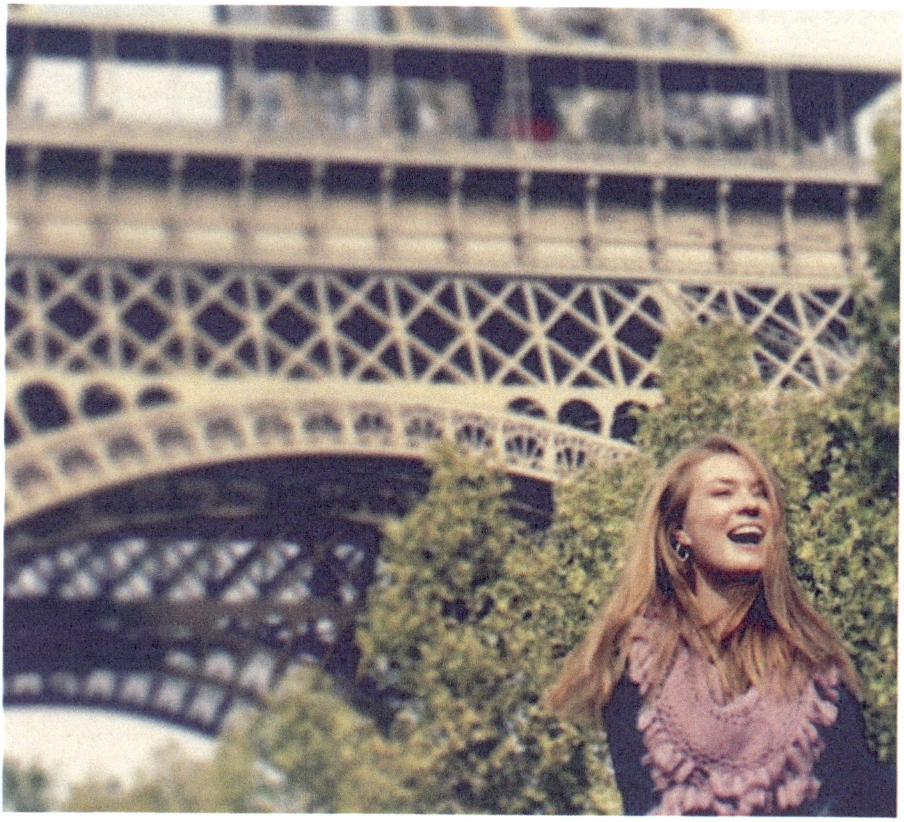

Module 3

Values, Mission, and Priorities

> "Far better it is to dare mighty things, to win glorious triumphs, even though checkered by failure, then to rank with those poor spirits who neither enjoy much nor suffer much because they live in that gray twilight that knows neither victory nor defeat."
>
> — Theodore Roosevelt

Objectives

At the end of this module, you will be able to:

- List your values and principles for living
- Identify your mission
- Write a letter to yourself from the future
- Determine which adventures are worth pursuing

Introduction

We are moving into the next phase of our journey and are building a foundation for future success. To get to the most important dreams, it helps to set some priorities. You can do most anything, yet, sadly, you cannot do everything at once. In this session, you will identify the values and principles for your life, creating a strong foundation for decisions about your future. You will establish a mission—your purpose in life— and determine which adventures are worth pursuing. This requires self-reflection and meditation.

What do you think Teddy is talking about in the quote on the previous page? Think about your great dreams; name one and go for it. Do not fear failure; it is only temporary and a stepping stone to learning how to win those "glorious triumphs."

Celebration and Review

Congratulations! You have written your dreams and created a vision board for your awesome life. You are open to what you once considered an impossible dream. You have drafted a vision for your future. Rhett demonstrated the power of putting your dreams to paper, and Kate shared the power of a vision board. When Kate created a vision, she felt hope and hope opened the door to opportunity. Your opportunities are unlimited! You may be experiencing enthusiasm about all the possibilities in your life or you may be feeling overwhelmed or somewhere in between. Don't worry—all is well.

The Hierarchy of Goals Triangle

This triangle depicts values and mission as a foundation for all visions, goals, and actions that will drive you towards your meaningful life. Your vision is the picture you hold of your future as far out as you can see. Though your vision changes to encompass new realities, opportunities, and dreams, your values will remain consistent over time. You will set long-range goals aligned to your vision, values, and mission and then break them down into bite-sized action steps. With each step, you come closer to achieving your goals, bringing your vision to fruition, and living your values and mission!

```
        /\
       /Action\
      / Steps  \
     /----------\
    /   Goals    \
   /--------------\
  /    Vision      \
 /------------------\
/  Values & Mission  \
----------------------
```

Module 3 — Values, Mission, and Priorities

Your Foundation

Values are your core beliefs or principles for living and guide your thoughts and actions. Values form the foundation for all our actions. They guide our decisions, our priorities, and our behavior. The voice of Jiminy Cricket tells us when we are straying from those values.

Your mission describes your purpose for living. List your strengths and gifts. Write down what the world needs. Your purpose lies in the intersection of your gifts and what the world is waiting for you to provide.

Your goals will be based on your vision and aligned with your values and mission. Each goal will be broken down into action steps.

Your Values

Your values describe the kind of person you want to be. These are ideals and none of us are perfect. We can, however, strive towards that ideal. Values help us to grow and inform our decisions, our actions, and our purpose. When we live in alignment with our values, we grow in self-esteem and confidence, and others see us as having integrity. When you know what is important to you, you are less likely to be persuaded by what other people say and do. You develop a deeper sense of self and are more resourceful in dealing with stress; you develop strong beliefs about what is important. You can disregard the things that do not align with your values. It's that Shakespeare thing! "To thine own self, be true." It's also the saying inscribed on the anniversary medallion earned by 12 Steppers— "To thine own self be true."

> *"All of us celebrate our values in our behavior."*
>
> **— John W. Gardner**

Follow a person around for a day, and you will see what they truly value, not what they espouse. We are all works in process. Benjamin Franklin kept a little black book to record how well he did living up to his espoused values. He would pick one value and at the end of the day, rate himself on how well he did. When he felt he had mastered that value, he picked the next value and rated himself on it. When he had completed his list of values, he started back at the beginning.

When you affirm your values, you affirm your self-worth and can more effectively handle threats to your sense of self. This reduces stress, increases well-being, improves academic performance, and enables you to be more open to behavioral change. Self-affirmation gained by focusing on your values reduces negative emotions and allows you to feel more resourceful.

As an example, let's examine a research study that demonstrated the effect of affirming values on weight loss through the lives of two women. Betty and Mary were trying to lose weight, so when given an opportunity to join a weight loss study, they both jumped at the chance. They suffered from stress by worrying about how they looked, what they ate, and how others viewed them. Betty joined the control group while Mary was in the experimental group. Mary, in the experimental group, was given a list of nine values and asked to write an essay about her most important value and why it was important to her. Betty, in the control group, was asked to write about her least important value and why it might be important to someone else. After ten weeks, Mary and others in the experimental group had lost more weight, had a lower body mass index (BMI), and a smaller waist circumference.[11]

Research shows when we think our values are important and we imagine positive future scenarios; we feel better about ourselves and get better results in desired behavior change. The neural pathways overlap and, on an MRI, show an increased response in the brain.[12]

Module 3 — Values, Mission, and Priorities

Identify the Values Most Important to You

Let's identify what principles of living are important to you. The list below includes values that others view as important. Review the list and pick those that resonate with you.

Circle or highlight the values most important to you. Feel free to add to this list. Select the top 7–10. Number them in order.

- Adventure
- Ambition
- Art
- Balance
- Beauty
- Comfort
- Community
- Compassion
- Courage
- Creativity
- Discipline
- Excitement
- Enthusiasm

- Family
- Forgiveness
- Freedom
- Friends
- Fun
- God
- Gratitude
- Health
- Humility
- Humor
- Independence
- Inner harmony
- Joy

- Justice
- Knowledge
- Leadership
- Love
- Openness
- Peace
- Pleasure
- Power
- Security
- Service
- Spirituality
- Wealth
- Willingness

Example — My top values
1. Spirituality
2. Love
3. Gratitude
4. Honesty
5. Enthusiasm
6. Health
7. Courage
8. Openness

Guided Imagery — Steps to All Knowing, All Loving, All Wise

Introduction to Guided Imagery

The following guided imagery is very short. The purpose of this guided imagery is to tap into your highest self to examine what values are most important to you. You can go inward at any time and ask for guidance, an intuitive thought or idea.

Steps to All-Knowing, All-Loving, All-Wise

Within you, there is a part of you that is all-knowing, all-loving, and all-wise. It is there as a resource to guide you. It may help if you imagine descending a flight of 10 steps which will lead you to this all-wise, all-loving and all-knowing place within you. All you need do is trust, choose, and be. Say to yourself, I trust that which is all-knowing, all-loving and all-wise. I choose that which is all-knowing, all-loving and all-wise. You allow your light to shine. You are powerful and wise. You deeply love and approve all that you are. Ask and the answers will come. What does the ideal you look like? ... What are those values or principles of living that mean the most to you? Who do you want to become? Ask, what is the most important thing for me to work on this year? In the next 3 months? Wait patiently for a response...

> *"I've learned that people will forget what you said, people will forget what you did; people will remember how you made them feel."*
>
> *— Maya Angelou*

Review your list of values and modify them as desired. You will be asked to write them out in complete sentences. The following is an example.

Module 3 — Values, Mission, and Priorities

Principles I Live My Life By — an Example of Personal Values

1. Spirituality—Be God-centered. Truly commit every day to God. Take the time to know and love God more and more every day. Grow in faith. Grow spiritually through prayer, meditation, reading and sharing with others.
2. Love—Love my family. Continually strive to build a closer relationship filled with love, respect, laughter, joy, and understanding. Help them to grow. Grow together spiritually.
   a. Love myself as I am. Grow in self-esteem, continually develop and maintain a strong sense of personal worth as I relate to myself and others. Strive to live congruently with my values yet show compassion towards myself when I don't.
   b. Love others. See God within everyone I meet. Find a seed of greatness within every person. Show warmth and compassion towards others. Help others to grow and get the results they desire out of life. Put others first, myself last.
3. Gratitude—Thank God for everything.
4. Honesty—Make commitments and stand by them. Be honest with myself and others. Live with integrity.
5. Enthusiasm—Be enthusiastic and positive. Have fun! Relax and enjoy life. Find humor in all situations.
6. Health—Be healthy. Strive to put only what is healthy into my body. Exercise daily.
7. Openness—Be open to goodness. Be able to accept gifts from God and others.

When I read my principles for living, I am reminded of what is important to me. My self-concept expands; I am more than a worker, a mother, a wife. Suddenly my monkey brain settles down and I can focus. Decisions are easier. I don't need to rush to those things calling for my attention; I can relax.

Now you try — List your top 7 values

1.
2.
3.
4.
5.
6.
7.

Module 3 — Values, Mission, and Priorities

Personal Values

Now write complete sentences about what you mean by each value. The values or principles I choose to live my life by:

Read your values daily!

Steps to Identify Your Mission   Example

1. What are your most important values and causes you care about?	• Spirituality • Helping people grow in recovery from addictions.
2. Identify the value you want to provide.	• Coach others to create and implement a compelling vision for success
3. Identify who you want to provide value.	• Individuals and organizations who want to improve and grow especially women in recovery.
4. Identify the skills that you are good at and give you joy.	• Leading others in guided imagery, facilitating workshops, designing training programs, coaching, planning

My personal mission

1. What are your most important values and causes you care about?	
2. Identify the value you want to provide.	
3. Identify who you want to provide value.	
4. Identify the skills that you are good at and give you joy.	

Module 3 — Values, Mission, and Priorities

Now fill in the blanks with the answers to 1–4 to create the beginning of a mission statement. Write your mission statement with the example below as a template.

The values and causes that are important to me are (1) _____

I want to help address this need through my mission in life by (2) _____

to (3) _____ through my skills in (4) _____

My Personal Mission Statement — Example

My purpose in life is to:

Help individuals and organizations create a compelling vision of what they can become, boldly follow their dreams, and achieve the results they want in life.

To live with love, joy, compassion, and courage, and to be an instrument of God.

Linda M Hogan

"My mission in life is not merely to survive, but to thrive; and to do so with some passion, some humor, and some style."

— **Maya Angelou**

"To ensure sustainable human development which encourages self-reliant and self-content society. To promote activities related to community services, social welfare and also Indian heritage and culture."

— **Mahatma Gandhi**

"I want to serve the people. And I want every girl, every child to be educated."

— **Malala Yousafzai, Nobel Prize laureate and activist**

Personal Mission

Now you try!

Story — David T. Lord

Introduction to David T. Lord

David T. Lord is one of the most mission driven people I know and I think you will find it interesting how his mission was revealed to him and what he did about it. Your path to discovering your mission will probably be different. Or maybe you already have a mission and don't realize it. Wayne Dyer told a story about a fish who was looking for the ocean. Every time he asked someone where the ocean was, he was told that he was already in it. "No," the fish responded, "I'm in the water; I am looking for the OCEAN!"

David T. Lord

While many people struggle to discover what their mission in life is, David T. Lord's mission has always been clear to him. The inspiration for his mission practically fell into his lap. One day while arranging some items on a shelf, a book toppled into his hands—one he hadn't noticed for a while. The book, *Process Consultation: Its Role in Organizational Development*, (published 1969) was written by Edgar H. Schein, Professor of Management Emeritus in the Sloan School of Management at the Massachusetts Institute of Technology. This inspired David, changed the trajectory of his career, and became the focus of a consulting business for over 30 years. David read Dr. Schein's book and put the principles into action. The book enabled David to lead business owners to improve their business processes. His mission? Helping your business work better.

I have experienced David's mission in action. It is 1993, I'm on a plane going from Detroit to Philadelphia. After taking off, I take out my laptop to review my presentation. The man sitting next to me asks what I'm working on and I tell him I'm preparing to meet a group of 40 plant managers for the first time and share the results of a learning needs assessment. The man next to me smiles, looks at his watch and says, "we have 2 hours 40 minutes; let's get to work!" He provides clarity and focus and boosts my confidence, what a godsend! He tells me his name, David T. Lord. Now I know — this really is one of God's messengers!

A few weeks later, David was in my office to help transform a blank wall into a system of visual management. I can now see exactly where each project is, what needs to be done, when it will be done, and by whom. Having fast, accurate access to information increased my team's effectiveness and enabled us to garner new respect from the company's leaders.

Sometime later, the Vice President of one of the businesses tells me that "Rome is burning"; his business is in serious trouble. We assess the needs and determine that we could save money by reducing scrap; we select three plants with the highest scrap rates and assign David and two colleagues to identify the extent of scrap. They used visual management and problem solving to identify the cause and extent of scrap, then engaged teams to problem solve the cause and eliminate it. Within three months we saved $280,000.

I have had more adventures with David, and he continues to impact my life and work. In 2013, David published *The Visual System of Work: Help Your Business Work Better, Make Money and Generate Cash: A 90 Day Implementation Guide*. In 2021, David published *The Visual System of Work Toolkit: Practical Tools to Help Business Get Better Fast*. He is now able to help even more businesseses work better!

Story — Dennis Archer

Introduction to Dennis Archer

The moment I met Dennis Archer, two-term mayor of Detroit from 1994–2001, I was impressed and inspired. The following is a short story focused on how he found his mission. I will share a longer story of Dennis Archer in Module 10.

Dennis Archer

Sometimes the mission comes first and then the vision follows. Dennis Archer was born January 1, 1942 in Cassopolis, a town of 1,500 people in southwest Michigan, in a home with a dirt floor and no indoor plumbing. Every month, the family made the 15-mile trip to the barber's, and it is here that he heard words that would be forever indelibly etched in his mind. The barber looked at the boy of 8–10 years old and said, "You are special. You are going to help a lot of people." The words and voice of the barber would pop into his head many times and influenced him to seek opportunities where he could be of service—to teach, practice law, serve on the Michigan Supreme court, lead the city of Detroit as mayor for two terms—finding time throughout to mentor numerous young people and then to establish a scholarship fund. He continues to be guided by that vision of providing service to others. Dennis Archer has had an incredible impact on numerous people. Archer told me that he wasn't sure if it was actually the voice of the barber or the voice of "the big guy upstairs." Throughout his life, Dennis Archer followed his mission to help as many people as he could. In Module 10, you will learn more about Dennis Archer and the impact he created.

Guided Imagery — The Meadow

Introduction to Guided Imagery — "The Meadow"

The Meadow guided meditation provides relaxation and healing. It is designed to tap into your intuition and spirituality.

The Meadow

You are walking along a path in a beautiful, green meadow. Feel the fresh air, a gentle breeze. See the colors of the flowers, the plants, wildlife ... Allow yourself some moments to freely explore the meadow as a child would ... going deeper into the meditation experience ... feeling more and more relaxed and childlike ... when you are ready for a rest, a blanket appears ... it looks so inviting ... lie on your back ... feel yourself relaxing deeply into the soft blanket ... and see the clouds ... notice the changing shapes ... notice any images ... or thoughts that come to your mind ... Find a brook with magical healing waters. Step into it ... the temperature feels good. Follow the brook ... There is some thought or emotion that is keeping you from reaching your goal. Imagine pouring that thought or emotion into the brook ... empty yourself of whatever holds you back. Here, you can be healed.

Continue along the path. You are about to have a special surprise, something deep within you has desired this for a long time. Remember you are in a magical place and this will be easy. Settle back and know that whatever scene you observe is right for you. See an image, a symbol, sound, or scene. All is well...

A path leads you to a gently rolling hill. As Meister Eckert said, "The path is beautiful and familiar and joyful and pleasant." A magical creature appears—the creature indicates that you should follow. It appears friendly with much wisdom. You follow and notice that you are walking, then skipping ... practically galloping ... then leaping like a gazelle ... You continue leaping with seemingly little effort ... As you look behind you, notice that you have been going higher and it is so easy. Now continue climbing, at your own pace ... whatever pace you choose, it is right for you ... you are now further up the mountain ... closer to your goal ... it is your mountain ... With each step, you can clearly see what step needs to be taken next ... Sometimes you seem to be walking down a gentle slope ... sometimes it may be more difficult ... you easily find the way over, under or around the obstacle ... you have developed your strength on this journey—

Physical strength ... spiritual strength ... Emotional and mental strength ... Your belief in yourself, in the journey and in your goal becomes stronger. Continue moving until you come to an obstacle that appears to be too much for you ... see it ... name it ... your magical creature will help—the magical creature guides you ... all you need to do is ask ... the creature tells or shows you the way through the obstacle ... see yourself moving through or by the obstacle as shown by your guide ... Imagine getting closer to the top ... you can see it clearly ... you move magically, gracefully ... now you are at the top ... Allow yourself some moments to thoroughly enjoy being at the top... notice the view ... take some time and look... you have some advice to yourself about overcoming obstacles to reach your goal ... reach for a piece of paper and pen and let the thoughts come through you, through the pen, onto the paper ... any other thoughts, perspectives about the journey or reaching the goal, any advice you would want to share—take some moments and write... then when you are ready to return to this time and place—see yourself in this room... notice the sound of my voice and on the count of three, gently open your eyes feeling alert and refreshed.

Guided Imagery Reflections

Take a few moments to jot down any thoughts or feeling that occurred to you during this meditation. Did anything surprise you? How did you feel? Were you able to ask for guidance?

Module 3 — Values, Mission, and Priorities

Story — Paulette

Introduction to Paulette

Paulette was a member of our first vision group in Albany, New York. I love how Paulette trusts her intuition and continuously, boldly follows her dreams. Paulette came to the United States from Switzerland in her early twenties to serve as a nanny for a family in New York City. Paulette is deeply spiritual, creative, and joyful!

Paulette

Paulette joined our visioning group in the early 1990's. The lease on her apartment was ending and she was searching for a new place to live. She was looking for a place that would remind her of home and would welcome her beloved cat. During our meditation, Paulette envisioned a place on a mountain lake like places she remembered from her native Switzerland. Apartment hunting continued; she saw a few cat-friendly apartments but did not find anything which reminded her of home. Paulette chose to trust her vision, to believe in its possibility, and did not lease any of the apartments she had seen. Her lease ended, and she had no place to go. She packed; she loaded the U-Haul and moved her boxes and furniture into a friend's garage. She shared her vision with a friend and the friend agreed to take her in until she found her dream place.

She called me on a Sunday and shared her excitement about finding her dream place in the hill town just outside a small city. She intuitively knew that this was the right place for her. But she was confused, this place was not on a lake, it did not fit her vision. We discussed the importance of trusting her intuition and she agreed to take the apartment.

When she went to get the keys to her new place, she realized that her apartment was a guest house. She checked her directions and proceeded down a path through the woods to the landlord's house. The path wound through pines and took her to a large pond. The landlord said that he sometimes swam in the pond. Paulette was a little disappointed: a pond, though beautiful, is not a lake. As she signed the check for the first month's rent the landlord exclaimed, "Oh, by the way, I forgot to tell you, across the street and behind the trees, there is a lake ideal for swimming. You have complete access to the lake."

By trusting her intuition, Paulette realized her vision. She had the place of her dreams. Paulette had other dreams; she imagined going to graduate school and becoming an art therapist. She went to study art in Boston and there met her future husband, who was also studying there and planning to return to his homeland—Switzerland.

Years later, I received the following in a letter from Paulette: "Amazingly, I am in the midst of realizing something I envisioned 20 years ago. I will be opening a private practice in art therapy. I will have my own studio in a therapy center that is opening July 1st. It is the dream of a psychiatrist to open this center. We will be around 20 professionals in the mental health field ranging from psychiatrists, psychologists, psychotherapist, me—an art therapist—and a few others. Bringing this project to life is a huge piece of work. I have done so much already that I have the feeling I am not far from a burnout, but yet I still need to write my fliers, put my website together, buy the furniture and material.

"Something I envisioned in your class is coming to birth right now." Ten years later, Paulette continues to enjoy her successful private practice.

Discussion

How did you feel about this story? What resonated with you? What did you learn about how this person created and implemented her vision? What could you apply?

Feelings	Thoughts that resonated with you
Action you will take	

Module 3 — Values, Mission, and Priorities

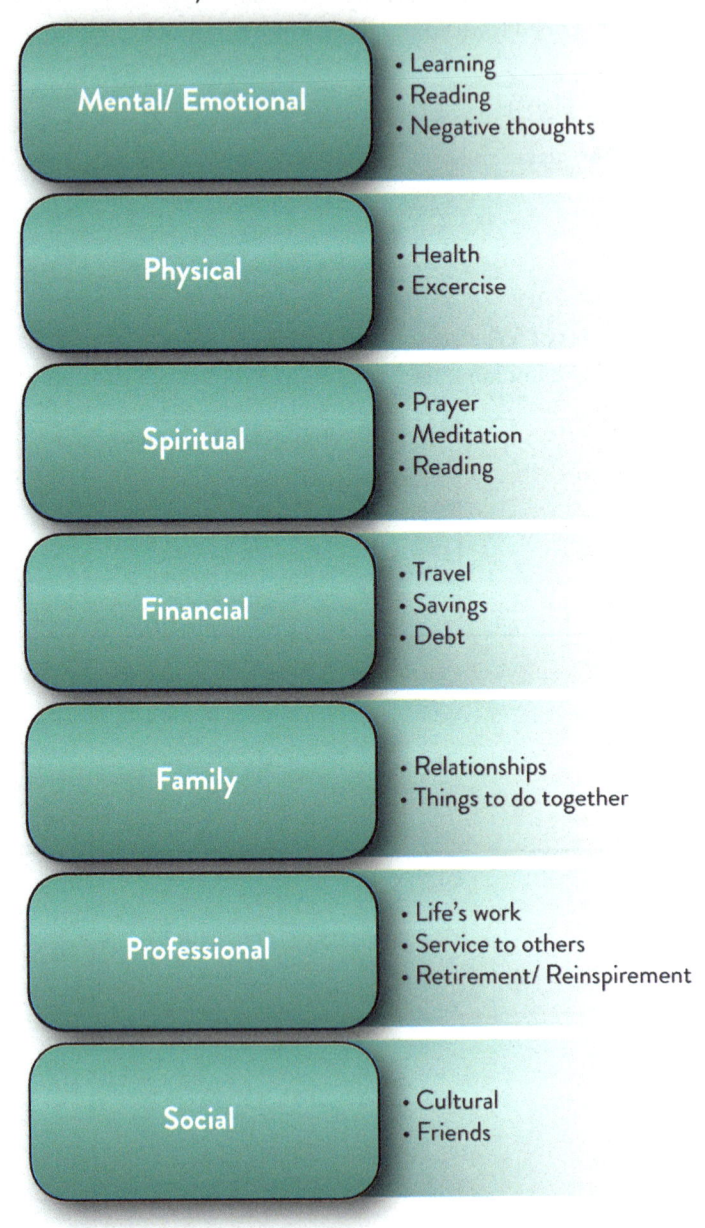

Setting Priorities in All Areas of Life

Review the list of "Areas of Life" and the examples listed to the right. Identify your top 3 areas of life that you want to work on now.

Mental/ Emotional
- Learning
- Reading
- Negative thoughts

Physical
- Health
- Excercise

Spiritual
- Prayer
- Meditation
- Reading

Financial
- Travel
- Savings
- Debt

Family
- Relationships
- Things to do together

Professional
- Life's work
- Service to others
- Retirement/ Reinspirement

Social
- Cultural
- Friends

Setting Priorities in all Areas of Life

Goals for Top 3 Areas of Life

Identify the three most important areas of your life. Now, set a goal for each area. Remember: your goals should be specific, difficult yet attainable, measurable, aligned with your vision and values, and have a due date.

1. Area	Goal
2. Area	Goal
3. Area	Goal

"Twenty years from now you will be more disappointed by the things you didn't do than by the ones you did do. So, throw off the bowlines. Sail away from the safe harbor. Catch the trade winds in your sails. Explore. Dream. Discover."

— Mark Twain

Module 3 — Values, Mission, and Priorities

A Letter from Your Future

Write a letter to yourself from the future in which you are fully living up to your vision and values as well as focused on your priorities. The three goals you just set have come to pass.

Describe the ideal future you are now living. Identify the date.

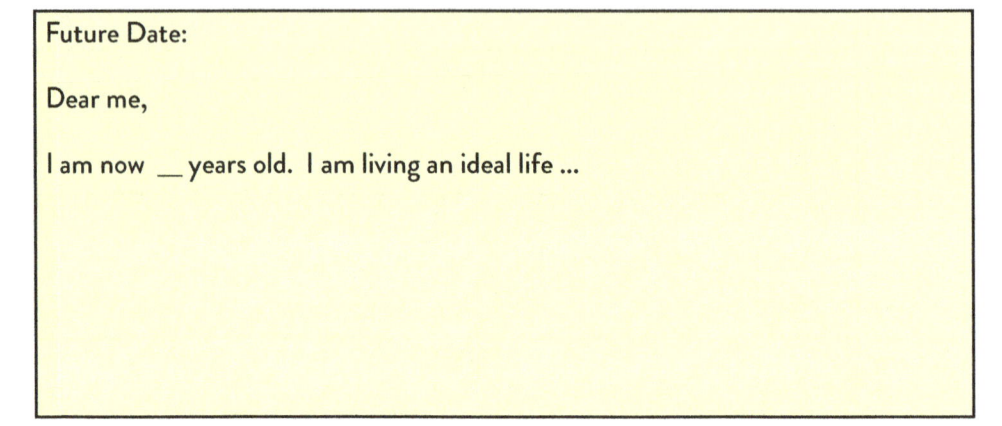

Future Date:

Dear me,

I am now __ years old. I am living an ideal life ...

> *"Planning is... attending to the goals we ought to be thinking about and never do, the facts we do not like to face and the questions we lack the courage to ask."*
>
> — John Gardner

What does the Research Say?

People who work for values- and mission-driven organizations are more committed and more likely to use discretionary time to achieve the organization's priorities. Individuals with a strong mission and values find it easier to make decisions and live with integrity. We admire people with integrity for upholding strong values, being consistent, and having a moral compass.

When we focus on our top values, stress reduces, learning improves, health improves; we don't need to defend ourselves from attacks on our self-concept because we know we are more than any one issue or self-concept. We are more resilient and can learn from feedback that would otherwise make us defensive.

This research is part of self-affirmation theory initially described by Claude Steele in the 1980's. [13] It states that we all want to have a positive view of ourselves and when this is threatened, we tend to get stressed and defensive. When we focus on our most important values, we have a greater perspective on who we are and our self-integrity is restored.

Action Steps

Directions: check each circle when completed:

1. Identify your top 3 areas of life. ○
2. Identify one or two goals in each of the top 3 areas of your life. These could include the 3 goals you already set for this program. ○
3. List your values / principles for living. ○
4. Draft a mission for your life. ○
5. Write a letter to yourself from the future. ○

Reflections

1. Journal on what gives you joy. Think about a time when you were happiest. ○
2. What are your greatest skills? What do you enjoy doing? What are your spiritual gifts? ○
3. What is your ideal for the world? What do you think the world needs from you? What can you do to contribute to that ideal world? ○
4. What is your mission? ○
5. What gift or legacy would you like to leave behind? ○

Module 4

Charting a Course

> "If you have built castles in the air, your work need not be lost; that is where they should be. Now put the foundations under them."
>
> — Henry David Thoreau, Walden 1854

Objectives

At the end of this module, you will be able to:

- Develop a plan to implement one of your goals aligned with your vision
- Learn how goal setting improves personal and organizational productivity
- Follow the steps of goal setting

Introduction

Now we are in the charting your course phase; we will take the goals you identified at the beginning of the program and increase your likelihood of success in accomplishing them. For over half a century, research has demonstrated the factors that improve the effectiveness of goals on performance. We will make your goals more effective to help you accomplish what you want in life.

Celebration and Review

You have made good progress! Let's review what we have accomplished. You have prepared for the journey, drafted a vision, and listed your dreams. You have set your mission, values, and priorities; this will serve as your foundation. Your commitment, self-esteem, and self-confidence have grown. Like Paulette, you are relying more on your intuition and are led by faith, not fear.

Factors that Influence the Effectiveness of Goals on Performance

As a consultant for 30 years to businesses and individuals, I learned when people consciously set goals, they improve their performance and productivity. I was curious about what factors would help make goals even more effective. For my master's degree thesis in Management Studies, I reviewed fifty-five research studies conducted over a twenty-year period and learned when specific factors are added to goals, goal setting has a more positive impact on performance than goals alone.

Why should you care? These powerful factors accelerate your goal achievement and help you achieve greater success.

The factors that improve the effectiveness of goals are:
1. Specific and clear
2. Difficult yet attainable
3. Feedback (knowledge of results)
4. Goal Acceptance/ Commitment
5. Belief
    a. Self-Efficacy
    b. Locus of Control
    c. Self-esteem
    d. Ability
6. Benefits of Achieving the Goal
7. Priming

Characteristics of the Goals

Specific and Clear — Do Your Best or Close Enough Does Not Work

Effective goals are specific and clear. A specific, clear goal defines the desired result. You must be able to see the goal in your mind's eye; and if you are asking someone else to complete the goal, their picture must match yours. Zack set a goal to be better at Excel. He was already using it to create basic spreadsheets. A year later, he still had not changed how he was using Excel. Then, he realized that what he wanted to do was use conditional formatting to display whether the business goals were on track or behind by showing a red, yellow, or green status on a monthly basis. He could see the format he wanted in his mind; it became specific and clear. Before, he didn't know what the goal meant; it was hazy and ambiguous. The person responsible for implementing the goal must clearly grasp what the goal means. Goals regulate behavior and hazy intentions lead to confusion and lowered performance.[14] Once you know what to do, you can determine how to do it and develop a plan of action. You clearly focus your attention and avoid wasting effort on unnecessary tasks.

Specific goals also lead to more consistent performance. Jean set a goal to do more strength training and listed all the exercises she wanted to do. She even tracked it whenever she did the exercises. However, she never stated how often she would perform the exercises and days went by without it. Later, she decided to do the arm exercise three times a week and the leg exercises two times a week. She became more consistent and her efforts showed results.

Difficult Yet Attainable — Feel the Challenge

Effective goals are difficult yet attainable. Set your goals as high as you believe you can achieve them and then just a little bit more beyond your grasp. Feel the challenge and believe you can succeed. The higher the goal level, the higher the performance level until the goal is impossible.[15] Of course, this assumes you have the ability to achieve the goal, you are persistent and committed to the goal, and you receive feedback on your progress. With specific, difficult goals you will work harder over time than if your goals were too easy. One of my very first dream lists included a marathon and at that time it was unattainable. I could run 3 miles. I set a goal to run 26.2 miles over a week's time on a regular basis. This was more than I was currently running, was a challenge but was attainable. Later, I set a goal to run a half marathon. Many years later, I set a goal to run a marathon and yes, it was difficult, but I attained it. I joined a marathon training group and we did our long runs together weekly. The support and camaraderie strengthened my commitment and belief that I could achieve the goal. I had a daily plan and I tracked my progress. And I ran my first marathon at 63!

In my work with a savings bank in New England, bank management established a goal for tellers to mention another product to 50% of the customers that came to their window. One of the branch managers was frustrated that one of her tellers was only cross selling to less than 5% of her customers. While the branch manager thought 50% cross sales was a reasonable target, the teller did not think it was realistic and gave up. They mutually agreed to a new goal of 10% and although the teller thought this was difficult, she thought she could do it. During the week, the teller mentioned other products to 10% of the customers. The goal level was gradually increased as the skills and confidence of the teller grew. Within three months, the branch manager reported that the teller was consistently mentioning the bank's other products to 60% of her customers!

How difficult are your goals? Do they motivate you to try harder? If not, make an adjustment, set them a little higher. You will adjust your effort to the level of goal difficulty.

Goal Acceptance/ Commitment

Goal acceptance and commitment have a positive effect on performance. Commitment requires a stronger emotional attachment to a goal. You commit to a goal when you keep it in front of you. Write it down! Share it with the people who accept you for who you are and support you. Sign your commitment to your goals. When you are committed to a goal, you persist despite the obstacles. When I committed to running a marathon, I went on long runs even if it was raining, snowing, freezing, or hot and humid. I ran at least 6 out of 7 days despite how I felt.

Intensity increases commitment. The time and mental effort I spent signing up for the marathon training group, planning my long runs, deciding on the pace, and problem solving when obstacles occurred, increased the intensity and therefore my commitment. I took action to accomplish the goal.

Performance Feedback (Knowledge of Results)

Feedback can be qualitative and subjective, "you are doing a good job." Through knowledge of results, feedback can be quantitative and measurable. To improve performance, feedback should be as specific and quantitative as possible. Feedback or knowledge of results provide information about how well or how poorly you are doing relative to your goal. It helps you know whether you are on track; you can see what you need to do to get back on track. You need to try harder or develop a different strategy to achieve the goal.[16] Feedback motivates a person to try harder[17]. Feedback provides more information to clarify the goal and increase knowledge of how to achieve the goal. The more specific the goal, the easier it is for feedback to be self-generated. When feedback is added to specific goals, performance improves.

Smart watches enable athletes to measure numerous factors that provide feedback on performance goals including distance, speed, heart rate, perceived effort, relative effort etc. I use real-time feedback on my pace and heart rate to try harder and improve performance.

When you set your goals, identify how you will know whether you are on track; are you winning or losing? Are you getting closer to your goal or further away? Make it a game and keep score. It can be exciting. We like sports because we can tell which team or athlete is winning and we can cheer for them.

Belief

When you set a goal, ask yourself, can I achieve it? You may ask this question while you are working on accomplishing a goal. If you believe you will accomplish the goal, you will persist despite the obstacles. When it gets difficult, tell yourself "I need to try harder" or "I must try a different strategy."

When you envision yourself already accomplishing your goal, your brain thinks that you have done it and belief increases. Athletes use this form of mental rehearsal to practice. My sister Deb, an Ironman competitor, envisions herself crossing the finish line and the timer displaying her goal time. She believes and achieves.

Self-Efficacy — "I think I can accomplish this task."

The adage, "if you think you can, you can, and if you think you can't, you can't," is true. Self-efficacy is a judgement one makes about how well they can competently perform the tasks required in a specific situation. Self-efficacy has a significant positive effect on performance. Albert Bandura has conducted numerous studies with people who: had phobias, quit smoking, had high stress, wanted to increase physical stamina, and had achievement goals. Your belief about your capabilities influence whether you will undertake a task and how confidently you will perform the task. It also determines how much effort you will expend and how long you will persist after encountering obstacles until you succeed. [18]

Researchers found that people who don't think they can meet a specific goal imagine personal deficiencies and potential difficulties as more insurmountable than they really are creating stress and impairing performance. In contrast, persons who have a strong efficacy focus their attention and effort to meet the demands of the situation and are motivated to greater effort by obstacles.[19] To obstacles, they say "bring it on!"

Locus of Control — "I am in charge."

Think about your goal, who will determine your success? Is it internal me or external them who will decide whether I succeed? Locus of control is an important psychological construct that identifies how a person perceives their actions and the impact they have on the external environment. Those with an internal locus of control believe they can have an impact on their environment and what happens to them. Those with an external locus of control believe circumstances, fate, or chance controls them and are responsible for what happens to them.

After a hurricane destroyed a New England city, many business owners lost their buildings and their businesses. Those who had an internal locus of control were far more successful in rebuilding their businesses over the next 5 years than those who believed that circumstances were out of their control.[20]

Self-Esteem — "I like me."

Self-Esteem has an inverse relationship to locus of control. People with high self-esteem have an internal locus of control and those with low self-esteem have external locus of control and believe that factors outside of themselves determine their success. People with high self-esteem are more willing to take on more difficult tasks and persist over a longer period of time. Build your self-esteem — set goals, envision success, and accomplish them.

Ability — "Do I know how or where I can learn how?"

Relevant knowledge, skills, and ability are essential in order to achieve most goals. Ability is not needed for easy goals, but as the difficulty increases to the impossible range, ability becomes significantly more relevant for performance[21]. When additional knowledge, skills, and ability are needed, set a learning goal to gain additional strategies to achieve the task.[22]

Core Self-Evaluation — "How do I view me?"

What if we put some of these factors together? We would have Core Self-Evaluation (CSE). Core Self-Evaluation, also called positive self-concept, is assessed on a Likert Scale with 12 items and identifies whether a person has a positive or negative self-evaluation. CSE is a combination of self-esteem, locus of control, self-efficacy, and emotional stability and predicts job satisfaction and job performance. Those with positive self-evaluation demonstrate higher job satisfaction and job performance than those with negative self-evaluation. [23]

Building belief is about building your core self-evaluation and empowering you to envision, believe, and accept the goodness you desire.

Benefits of Achieving the Goal — "I will get something out of this!"

Working hard and long on a goal can become daunting or just plain frustrating. There must be something in it for you to achieve the goal. Imagine a scale with the work required on one side and the benefits for achieving on the other side. The more benefits you can add, the more worthwhile the goal becomes and your desire increases. Break your goals down into easy to do tasks and give yourself rewards for your effort and progress on a regular basis. I like to reward myself with a little snack after so many hours of work. Motivate yourself with a treat that works for you.

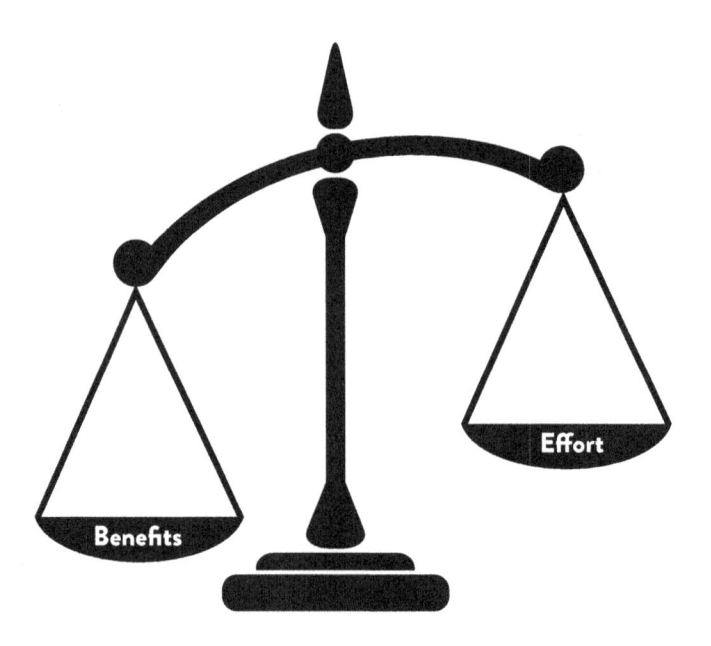

Priming

Goals primed in the unconscious (by seeing a picture or a movie of a person being successful, such as in winning a race) have the same effect on performance as those consciously set. Priming the pump increases our odds of achieving the goal.[24] We prime the pump every time we vividly imagine ourselves achieving the goal or look at our vision boards. Remember times in the past when you persistently strived to achieve a goal and you will increase your persistence on your current goal. The work you are doing in this program to define, prioritize, and reflect on the importance of your goals increases your achievement in other areas of life.

Steps to Goal Setting
1. Set specific goals.
2. Identify benefits of attaining your goals. Create desire.
3. Identify rewards for making incremental progress.
4. Identify obstacles.
5. Generate solutions.
6. Identify action steps.
7. Set target dates.
8. Build belief.
9. Measure progress.
10. Sign your commitment.

Module 4 — Charting a Course

Examples of Specific Goals

Specificity builds success!

General Unclear Goals	Specific Goals
Go to Europe.	I will go to France, Italy, and Germany by September 2030 for 3 weeks. Identify the specific cities in which you will start and end to make it more specific.
Buy a new house.	I will purchase a new home in Great City, USA in the $400,000 – $450,000 range by June 2025 with the help of a realtor. Identify the school you want to be near to make it more specific.
Sell my current home.	I will sell my current home for more than my asking price within 3 days of putting it on the market.
Lose weight.	I will lose 7 lbs. in the next 30 days. I will keep a food diary.
Remember the birthdays of friends and people in my extended family.	Make a list of birthdays by month. During the last week of the month purchase birthday cards for the next month, address, sign and mail a few days before the birthday.
Exercise more.	I will do a cardio exercise at least 3 times per week for 40 minutes each time. This could include running, bicycling, swimming, or elliptical.
Reach out more to friends.	I will call 3 friends every day and have lunch or coffee with one each week.

Checklist for Effective Goals

Use this to evaluate whether your goals are clear and specific.

Characteristics of Good Goals	Check is Yes
1. You can see the goal in your mind and know exactly what to do.	
2. You have a target date for accomplishing the goal.	
3. A little beyond your reach but still possible to attain.	
4. You are committed to achieving this goal.	
5. You are tracking progress and can tell if you are winning or losing.	
6. You believe you can and will achieve the goal despite external circumstances.	
7. You can see what's in it for you and the benefits motivate you to work towards the goal.	
8. You practice seeing yourself in possession of my goal.	
9. You affirm positive beliefs about being in possession of your goal.	
10. You take continuous action to achieve your goal.	
11. You break your goals down into steps.	

Module 4 — Charting a Course

Goal Worksheet

Today's Date

Target Date

SMART Goal (**S**pecific, **M**easurable, **A**ttainable, **R**ealistic, **T**ime Bound)
Difficult Yet Attainable

> **SMART Goal**
> Describe the goal as clearly and specifically as possible.

> **Target Date**
> Identify the date for achieving your goal. If you are not making the progress you would like to be making, cut your goal in half and double the amount of time needed to complete it.

Benefits (Create desire)

> **Benefits from achieving the Goal**
> Why do you want to achieve this goal? What is in it for you? This will increase your focus and motivation to attain the goal.

Identify rewards for making incremental progress.

Obstacles

> **Obstacles**
> Obstacles are problems and problems are opportunities. List all the obstacles to accomplishing your goal. To gain greater clarity on your obstacles, ask "why" 5 times.

Solutions

> **Solutions**
> Problems help clarify thinking and clear thinking helps identify solutions.

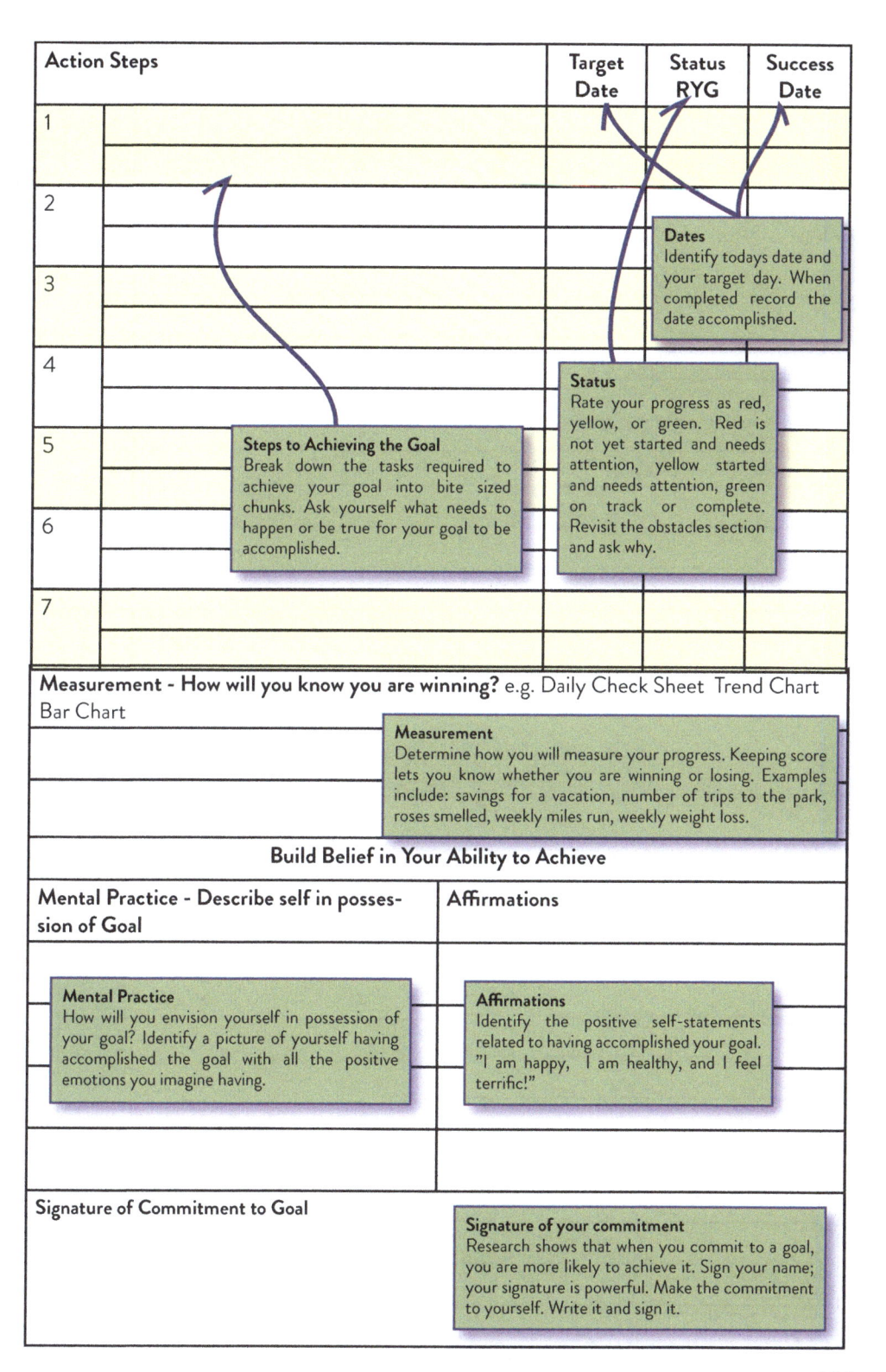

Action Steps		Target Date	Status RYG	Success Date
1				
2				
3				
4				
5				
6				
7				

Dates
Identify todays date and your target day. When completed record the date accomplished.

Steps to Achieving the Goal
Break down the tasks required to achieve your goal into bite sized chunks. Ask yourself what needs to happen or be true for your goal to be accomplished.

Status
Rate your progress as red, yellow, or green. Red is not yet started and needs attention, yellow started and needs attention, green on track or complete. Revisit the obstacles section and ask why.

Measurement - How will you know you are winning? e.g. Daily Check Sheet Trend Chart Bar Chart

Measurement
Determine how you will measure your progress. Keeping score lets you know whether you are winning or losing. Examples include: savings for a vacation, number of trips to the park, roses smelled, weekly miles run, weekly weight loss.

Build Belief in Your Ability to Achieve

Mental Practice - Describe self in possession of Goal	Affirmations
Mental Practice How will you envision yourself in possession of your goal? Identify a picture of yourself having accomplished the goal with all the positive emotions you imagine having.	**Affirmations** Identify the positive self-statements related to having accomplished your goal. "I am happy, I am healthy, and I feel terrific!"

Signature of Commitment to Goal

Signature of your commitment
Research shows that when you commit to a goal, you are more likely to achieve it. Sign your name; your signature is powerful. Make the commitment to yourself. Write it and sign it.

Module 4 — Charting a Course

Goal Worksheet

Today's Date

Target Date

SMART Goal (**S**pecific, **M**easurable, **A**ttainable, **R**ealistic, **T**ime Bound)
Difficult Yet Attainable

Benefits (Create desire)

Identify rewards for making incremental progress.

Obstacles	Solutions

Action Steps		Target Date	Status RYG	Success Date
1				
2				
3				
4				
5				
6				
7				

Measurement - How will you know you are winning? e.g. Daily Check Sheet Trend Chart Bar Chart

Build Belief in Your Ability to Achieve	
Mental Practice - Describe self in possession of Goal	Affirmations

Signature of Commitment to Goal

Module 4 — Charting a Course

Guided Imagery — Teddy Bear Picnic and Your Inner Child

Introduction to Guided Imagery

The next guided imagery will take you on a journey of fun and relaxation; you will visit a fanciful place where Teddy Bears do go on picnics... and you are invited!

Teddy Bear Picnic and your Inner Child

Imagine a late summer day ... the sun is warm, blue sky, some light fluffy clouds ... A path appears and you follow the path. You are relaxed and peaceful ... the path winds down a hill and as you continue you become more relaxed. You feel safe and secure. Notice the beautiful flowers and trees ... The path is now winding around, and you can see that you are quite high and that the path continues to wind down taking you to a beautiful place ... In the distance you can see a large pink blanket. As you get closer, you see that this is no ordinary blanket. You know that on journeys such as this magic seems to happen. The blanket is light and fluffy and appears to be many times the size of an ordinary blanket. You are still some distance away. Continue on the path. You are curious and want to explore ... You are reaching closer to the blanket. The blanket is warm and inviting .... Sit or lie down ...Feel the texture of the blanket ... You have the feeling that you need do nothing ... Everything you need you already have ... Listen .... Is that music you hear? ... Look where it is coming from .... You can't quite make it out, but the sounds are pleasant and joyful ... As you continue to look, the music becomes gradually louder ... You see that it is a group of Teddy Bears. They seem very friendly, so you stay where you are. Some of the Teddy Bears' are playing instruments. Some are carrying food ...They lay out a banquet of food. Anything you could want is there. You smell the food and turn your attention to that buffet. the food has been laid out and a Teddy Bear hands you a plate. Fill it up and enjoy. It is delicious! The Teddy Bears are eating too! Then ... All the food and the plates get cleaned up and magically disappear ...Watch the Teddy Bears, their antics and laughter .... You can feel their joy ... One of them tells you that your dreams are like a buffet of choices. Anything you want is there for your choosing ... In a flash you see all the possibilities for your future ... relationships, your adventures, your contributions to others ... the gifts that you bring ... money and the things that money can buy ... Pick the things that bring you joy and love ....You notice something you hadn't seen before ... we should say someone ... a little girl is here with the teddy bears. You feel an instant connection with her ...Shyly, she walks over to you and pulls on your sleeve ... She looks a lot like you ....your heart opens to welcome her here ...she seems very wise. She has a message for you ... she tells you what she wants or needs from you ... listen ... You thank her from the bottom of your heart ... Satisfied, she disappears ... It has been an amazing day! You stretch out on the blanket and go to sleep ... After some time you awake as you do any other day. You are home ... the sun is coming through your window and it is time to get up ... hear my voice. Feel the chair you are seated on ... Feel your fingers and wiggle them ... Wiggle your toes and gradually come back to this room and when you are ready, gradually open your eyes.

Guided Imagery Reflections

Take a few moments to jot down any thoughts or feeling that occurred to you during this meditation. Did you meet your inner child? What did they have to share with you? Did anything surprise you? How did you feel?

Story — Calvin

Introduction to Calvin

The Michigan Minority Business Development Council supports the development of relationships between the minority business owners and leaders of large corporations. These relationships lead to increased contracts for minority business owners and enable the large corporations to cultivate a supply base that mirrors their customers and provides a competitive advantage. I was impressed with the leadership of Calvin and was inspired by his story. I think you will be inspired too!

Calvin

Through my work with the Michigan Minority Business Development Council, I was given the opportunity to facilitate a strategic planning session for the National Association of Minority Contractors in Milwaukee. During the planning, I led 20 men in a guided imagery of their desired future for the association. Each person in turn shared part of their vision, wrote it on a sticky note, and posts on the flip chart. We created a storyboard of their powerful, collective vision. Afterwards the leader of the group, Calvin, approaches me and shares, "I believe that you can consciously effect your destiny. It has helped me create an amazing life!"

Later, I learned more about this amazing, visionary man. Calvin has envisioned and realized numerous dreams. Where others would become discouraged and feel victimized, he sees what is and imagines the opposite. He thinks through the possible risks and problems and imagines handling them using a positive attitude, perseverance, and sound strategies. "It is important to believe in your spiritual self," he says. He believes that God's spirit works through him. "I am a vessel. The power comes from God." Calvin advises those who have no dreams or hopes for the future to "believe in your spiritual self, that you are connected, that it will happen. If you believe it can happen, it will happen. It is okay to dream; then you need to set goals and determine how to get there. You must make it a challenge, don't stop yourself. Read the literature; learn what others have done. Search out knowledge to fortify yourself. Try to get better."

Calvin graduated from high school and had no money to go to college, but in his mind's eye—he was already there. He envisions being in college and was not surprised when the Urban League awarded him a full scholarship to the University of Pittsburgh. He majored in communications with minors in English and Black Studies and envisions himself with a career in mass media. He went on to have four radio stations, a TV station, and a national publication, the Minority Business Journal.

While studying at the university, Calvin interned with an ABC affiliate, gaining hands-on experience in a newsroom and then interned in cable television. He was drafted to be on a committee to represent the black community. Blacks were marginalized with no power, no voice. So, Calvin envisioned the opposite, he visualized Black people having a significant role in the legislature, in finance, and in the community. Through community action, this came to pass; Black people in Pittsburgh owned 20% of the businesses.

He wanted to involve African Americans in a listener-controlled station. He envisionseda good jazz show on Sundays with good information for the community in Pittsburgh; people were listening to his commentary with soft jazz in the background. He called the show "Sable Vibes and Expressions," then had "Sable Conversations" on Saturday. This grew to 20 hours of programming. He auditioned at a TV station and got his own TV talk show where he encountered people from all walks of life. Calvin was disturbed by the injustice he saw and spoke out. He became concerned and thought that he might need to have enough money to hire a lawyer, or... he could become a lawyer. He read business and financial books and magazines and visualized himself as "a crack businessperson" but recognized that he couldn't read legal jargon. So, he visualized himself getting into law school and practicing law; then did that for 10 years. He envisioned being a publisher. He combined his skills with passion to promote minority businesses. He thought that a publication with advertising would make money. He visited a person at the Pittsburgh Courier to seek advice. This person became his partner in the Minority Business Journal, shedding new light on minority businesses. After 5 years, he sold his share back to his partner.

Next, Calvin envisioned a successful contractors' association that secured business for minority contractors. They obtained 10% of the business from a major project in Milwaukee and increased contracts with the Department of Transportation in the state.

Calvin learned the importance of being credible to those who can affect his dream. If you reason with people and share with them, they will trust you. Listen, be humble, be honest, not conniving, be positive and constructive. Respect others and dialogue with them. Vision is seeing the possibility of the future.

Discussion

How did you feel about this story? What resonated with you? What did you learn about how this person created and implemented his vision? What could you apply?

Feelings	Thoughts that resonated with you

Action you will take

What does the Research Say?

Gary Latham and Edgar Locke independently studied the impact of goal setting on significantly improving individual and organizational performance. In 1974, they joined forces and their research partnership has continued to this day. They summarize the research in a 2019 chapter published by the American Psychological Association: "The Development of Goal Setting Theory: A Half Century Retrospective." For the past 50 years, research has demonstrated that goal setting improves performance regardless of task, participants, nationality, goal source, setting, experimental design, level of analysis (individual, team, organizational) and time span. Their work integrates hundreds of studies across thousands of participants. [25]

Module 4 — Charting a Course

Action Steps

Directions: check each circle when completed:

1. Identify your top 3 goals for the next 90 days. ○
2. Complete the goal sheet for 3 of your top goals for the next 90 days to one year. ○
3. Start tracking your progress. ○

Reflections

1. What aha's did you have regarding the research in goal setting? ○
2. How did it feel to complete the goal sheet? ○
3. What was the most difficult part? ○

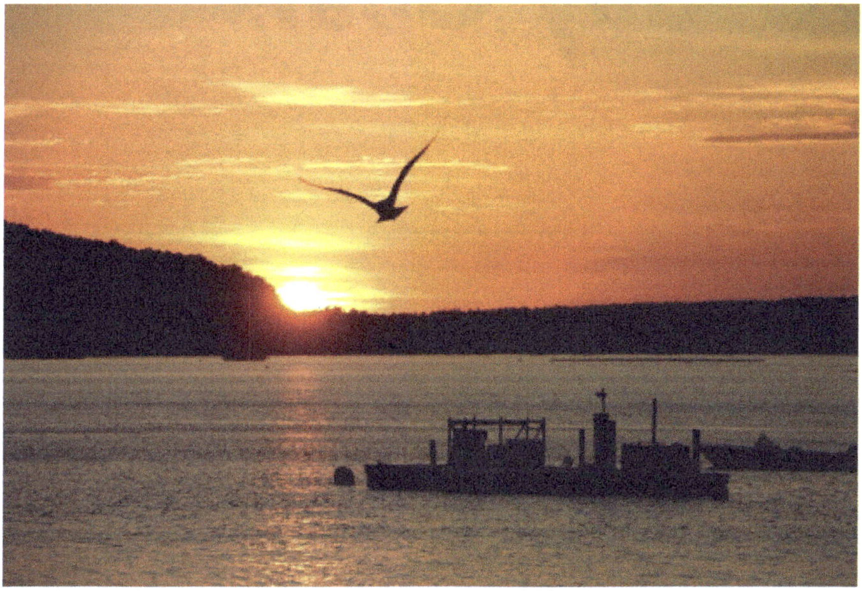

Module 5

Achieving Your 90-day Goals

Objectives

At the end of this module, you will be able to:

- Awaken and expand your intuition
- Identify 3 goals for the next 90 days
- Make your goals more concrete
- Incorporate mental practice and affirmations
- Implement strategies to help you achieve your goals

> *"Life is a process of becoming more conscious of the unique person we are. Development is a lifelong journey towards wholeness."*
>
> *— Carl Jung*

Introduction

Your long-range goals are aligned to your vision, mission, and values. You will narrow your focus by setting shorter-range goals until you know what you need to do each day to bring them to reality. We will expand your awareness and development of your intuition, helping you to rely on it more fully to make decisions that are right for you. You hold the goal firmly in your mind, yet let go and let God take care of the outcome.

Celebration and Review

Congratulations! You have completed the hard work of crystallizing your goals for the future. Your belief in yourself and your goals is growing. We learned from Calvin the importance of believing in your spiritual self and if you believe it, it will happen. Every step you take is progress and brings you closer to your goals. You've got this!

Awakening Your Intuition

You have done the work to create a vision. While you worked to expand your dream list and set goals, you may have experienced the inner way of knowing, the prompting or still small voice of your intuition. The Merriam-Webster dictionary defines intuition as "the ability to know something without any proof or evidence."

The phone rings and you know who is calling before you answer. You have a bad feeling about a trip and avoid it, only later discovering you might have been in an accident. You meet a person and have a positive feeling about that person. How did you know these things?

How has intuition worked in your life? What experiences have you had?

I had to go to Mexico for work and had put my passport in a four-drawer file cabinet (we used to have those things). I opened each drawer and looked through the folders patiently at first, then, increasingly frustrated, I went through the drawers a second time, then desperately a third. I was crying. I was beside myself. I walked away. I prayed for help. Immediately I saw in my mind's eye, the passport nestled in the first folder of the top drawer. I serenely and confidently went to the cabinet and opened the first drawer. There was my passport; it was nestled in a folder set snuggly against the inside front of the top drawer.

Why Develop Intuition?

Develop your intuition and you will see more possibilities and more choices. You will develop more creativity and be able to innovate. Your decision making will be enhanced, and you will increase your conscious contact with God. Weston H. Agor interviewed numerous leaders and found that intuition is an increasingly important skill for leaders. It is especially useful in decision making in times of uncertainty, where facts are limited, time is limited, and pressure is on to make the right decision, where there are many possible solutions and facts can support any option.[26]

Increasing Intuition

To increase your intuition, you must first set an intention and then listen. Quiet the mind through meditation, relaxation, and guided imagery. Let go and let God. Identify a question or information you seek. Hold it loosely in your mind. Try journaling and spiritual writing by allowing your higher power to answer the question. Observe any thoughts or images that come up. Notice synchronicities. Notice the difference between the ego pushing and shouting and the gentle nudge of intuition, the still small voice within. Mentally — notice your passions. Emotionally pay attention to your feelings. It must "feel right." Physically — notice a stillness, a grounding, a certainty. Spiritually — listen.

Guided imagery is an excellent way to develop your intuition by accessing the unconscious.

Spiritual Writing

Research shows that meditation and guided imagery block the sense of self, allowing one to bypass the ego and reach the subconscious. While in a meditative state, prayerfully request guidance from your higher power. Ask questions, start writing, and the answers will come to you. This is spiritual writing.

Listening to Intuition

New Job at Johnson Controls

It is 1992, GE Plastics has decided to reduce all contractors' fees by 10% and New York State has decided they will renegotiate all contracts. These are my two major customers and the future does not look bright. My husband suggests I apply for a job. He brings home the National Employment Weekly, a paper published by the Wall Street Journal and shows me ads for three jobs. One of the jobs requires experience in the plastics industry. The ad seems to glow and I exclaim: "I have 3 years' experience at

GE Plastics! That is a job for me." I submit my resume. I receive a call from the hiring manager, who announces that she is sitting there with a two-foot stack of resumes and "yours just floated to the top." We have a great conversation with great rapport. She asks what my salary requirements are, and an inner voice prompts me to say $60,000, much more than I have netted in my business. "I want you to come to Michigan for an interview. I will send you the airline tickets." I am so excited. I know this job is mine. It feels so right.

Three days later, I receive a voicemail from the hiring manager. She says that they have changed direction and she no longer wants me to come for the interview. "Send the airline tickets back." She says. How can this be? I have a deep knowing that this is the right job for me and I am the right person for the job. I return the call and tell her that if it is about the money, I will take less. I want this opportunity! I go to the interview and am impressed by the people who interview me, the company, and the Automotive Group headquarters in Plymouth, Michigan. The hiring manager says "we like you and you like us. We want you to be the Manager of Training for $60,000; when can you start?" This is the exact amount I had stated during the phone interview. I am so grateful for the intuition that urged me to apply and gave me the courage to not accept the request to send the tickets back. It is May 1992 and we move to Ann Arbor Michigan. It is the first week on the job and as I am entering the long corporate driveway, I hear an inner voice say, "thank you for trusting, my child." I am overwhelmed with gratitude.

New Assignment as Executive on Loan

It is 2003, I am on my way to work, listening to National Public Radio. The Governor of Michigan is asking corporations to identify executives to loan to the state government to implement productivity and quality improvements in the public sector. I experience a little burst of excitement. That still small voice says this would be fun! I had returned from a European assignment about a year earlier and was not challenged in my current position. I had led the creation of productivity improvement programs such as lean manufacturing and Six Sigma in over 15 countries in Europe. I would be a great consultant to the government. It suddenly occurred to me that I must speak to Chuck, the Vice President of Human Resources about this opportunity. As I enter the building, Chuck is coming out of an office to my right and I fall into step beside him. I tell him what I heard and how I would love to be an executive-on-loan. He says, "Coincidentally, the President of the Michigan Minority Business Development Corporation called me yesterday and asked me to appoint an executive-on-loan." His enthusiasm picks up, "I hadn't thought of you but now that you bring it up, you would be a perfect choice. They could use someone of your talents to help minority businesses improve their performance." The next week I drove to work at the Fisher

Building in downtown Detroit to start my assignment as Executive-on-Loan at the Michigan Minority Business Development Council. Was it a coincidence, or a God-incidence?

Guided Imagery — Intuition: Letting Go and Letting God

Introduction to Guided Imagery

The purpose of the next guided imagery is to enable you to access your intuition. Find a comfortable place to sit. During this guided imagery, you will invite your intuition to provide guidance. If you have a question, hold it loosely in your mind.

Intuition: Letting Go and Letting God

Take a deep breath. And another deep breath. Allow your abdomen to rise and fall. As your breathing becomes slow and even you will feel more and more relaxed. Now relax your whole body in stages by whatever works for you. You will feel mentally alert and stay mentally alert. You are in control. Your body will feel warm and heavy. Deepen this feeling of relaxation by slowly counting backwards from 10 to 1. 10, 9, 8, 7, 6, 5, 4, 3, 2, 1

Go to your special, sacred space and let yourself totally relax. I will give you a few moments to create that space. View your surroundings and make any adjustments needed to make yourself feel more comfortable and peaceful. This is where you can experience all that is good, loving, and wise. You are here to connect to God and to become your highest self for good in the world. Matter, time, and space are unlimited...

You can let go of anything blocking you from living happy, joyous, and free. Perhaps useful in the past, you no longer need these. Let it go... You can give them to your higher power. See yourself doing so ... You will feel lighter ... Feel the sun ... Feel the sun coming through the top of your head and into every cell in your body — healing and relaxing you ... clearing all blocks ... feeling love radiate throughout your body ... Feel the love in your heart extending outward ... to your family ... friends... the community ... the world ... Feel connected to everyone and everything ... Feel connected to your higher power ... Your intuition is strong. You are ready to receive guidance ... Listen to the still small voice of intuition. Allow any images to come and go. Simply note the voice or image that appears. Ask a question and listen ... a thought or idea will emerge.

Allow your mind to become clear and focus on a person, place, or event about which you wish to have more information... Look attentively at this image. Now wait passively for other images to appear. Simply note the images that appear and accept them as relevant information. When you return to this room, you will remember these images or words. To return, count slowly to 10. Gently move some part of your body. Allow yourself to return slowly and open your eyes when you feel ready. You will feel rested and calm yet alert and ready to interpret what you have seen and heard ....

Guided Imagery Reflections

Take a few moments to jot down any thoughts or feelings that occurred to you during this meditation. Did anything surprise you? How did you feel? What blocks you from living happy, joyous, and free? Were you able to let them go?

Story — Teri

Introduction to Teri

I met my friend Teri in Ann Arbor, Michigan after I returned from four years in Germany. We were both from New York State and her enthusiasm and zest for life uplifted me. Teri often dropped by our home and was a frequent dinner guest. She loves Bill's pizza and raspberry-apple pie.

Teri

It is 2021. At a Women's Vision workshop, I lead the participants through the process of creating a vision for their future in the next 10 years using guided imagery and creating vision boards. I have them go through magazines and cut out pictures and words that represent their ideal future, then paste them into a collage. Teri, who had recently completed her post-doctoral work, creates a beautiful vision board. In it, she has a home, a handsome husband, children, and a wonderful dog. She is spiritual and her work is meaningful. None of this is physically evident. Yet, she has set the future in motion.

Shortly thereafter, she gets a fantastic job with a chemical company in New York. Initially, all is well. Then, the role changes and challenges ensue. Teri travels to Virginia to visit me and my family for a weekend. Usually positive and upbeat, Teri is extremely unhappy with her job at the pharmaceutical company and complains about her manager. She is miserable, absolutely unable to bear this situation any longer; she is desperate to find a way out. We talk about God, letting go, and getting out of the way so that God can work miracles.

My husband Bill asks Teri when she was happiest, and she tells us about Brent and how in love they were; they were engaged to be married over twenty years ago. This is the first time we had heard about Brent. Bill gives directions to her home in New York through Pennsylvania to avoid the DC traffic and she follows them.

On Monday, Teri returns to work and is told that due to business conditions, she must be let go. She is shocked and relieved. On Wednesday, Teri receives a Facebook friend request from Brent, whom she has not had contact with for over 20 years. They message back and forth, talk on the phone, then meet where Brent lives in Reading, Pennsylvania, a city that Teri passed through on her trip home from my house. Brent has been divorced for five years and has a 15-year-old son. They fall in love again and in October, they marry. I know, it is amazing!

Today, they live in a beautiful home with two children and a dog. Teri is doing meaningful work in the community and leads a spiritual life.

From Teri, "Please use it, especially if it can inspire others. In a way, it's not mine to keep!!! The other day I was going through boxes (ha, prepping for our next move) and came across my vision board (I still have it!!!). The vision work that I did all those years ago demonstrates how powerful God is and how the plan for our lives is embedded in our hearts/mind. I think it was you that told me once that if I could "see it," it would be done. Something like ownership of what was already there in my heart. It has been a gift to be an active participant (due to sobriety) in life unfolding! Every. Single. Thing. on my board, has come to fruition! It's time to do another one. The only thing you "forgot" is my own office—and you said to dream big—so I wanted an office with windows and a pleasant view. BAMM… I had a beautiful tree that changed magnificent colors in the autumn and housed bird nests in the spring and summer. Life is good."

Discussion

How did you feel about this story? What resonated with you? What did you learn about how this person created and implemented her vision? What could you apply?

Feelings	Thoughts that resonated with you

Action you will take

Identify Your Top Three goals.

Refer to your three goal sheets and update them if needed. During this session, we will work on making your goals more specific for the next 90 days.

1.

2.

3.

Mental Practice

Mental practice is a powerful tool that will set unseen events in motion to make your vision a reality. Think of an important goal you want to achieve. You are going to powerfully embrace your goal. Visualize yourself in possession of your goal with all the emotions of achievement. This mental practice works best when you involve strong positive emotions, see it in vivid color, and use as many senses as possible. See yourself talking and listening to others talking about your success. See yourself in action. You will notice opportunities that will take you closer to your goal. You will develop confidence and the belief that you will realize this goal.

We know how to set a goal; we have written our goals. We have intellectually embraced our goals, now we will emotionally embrace our goals.

Research showed that mentally imagining something has a far greater impact on emotions than simply verbally processing an event or describing it. Other research demonstrates that repeatedly imagining a positive future leads to increased feelings of optimism.

World Golf Hall of Famer Annika Sorenstam shares that the most important thing that golfers need to control is between their ears. While in the think box, she calculates wind speed, distance and other variables, then visualizes the perfect shot. She cautions people to not remember their worst shot. Once the best shot is clearly in mind, move into the play box, empty your mind, address the ball, and swing. Think before you play, Annika Sorenstam advises New England golfers (Golf Content Network).

When asked whether she uses visualization, Sorenstam replied, "Absolutely. I always considered my mind my 15th club. Not only with positive thoughts and vision, but also with course strategy and playing to my strengths. I took great pride in thinking my way around the golf course," (Sorenstam on Clubs, Mental Game, & Swedish Food • Women's Golf Journal). [27]

Guided Imagery — Visualizing a Specific Goal

Introduction to Guided Imagery

When you envision a specific goal, you are practicing achieving that goal and the positive result. This increases your confidence and your belief that you will achieve the goal. You will try harder and persist despite any obstacles. You will recognize opportunities to help you reach your goal. The more you practice, the more success you will have!

Visualizing a Specific Goal

Relax ...

You are now in possession of your goal. See yourself in possession of your goal. See clearly what it looks like. Feel the emotions you will feel when you have attained the goal. You can make the picture more specific. As you change it, check how you feel ... For example, you may want to make the goal bigger or smaller. Adjust the size until you feel better. Notice the room you are in. Make it more pleasant. If you have a negative emotion, you have a choice—change what you are seeing or change the emotion to experience joy, serenity, love, or whatever positive emotions you would like to experience. Hear the positive things others say ... See yourself with your goal achieved in action. Make the colors brighter ... See yourself in sharper focus ... Involve as many senses as possible: smell your success, touch your success.

Guided Imagery Reflections

Take a few moments to jot down any thoughts or feelings that occurred to you during this meditation. Did anything surprise you? How did you feel? What positive things were said about you?

Affirmations

Affirmations are positive self-statements. Many of us hear an internal dialogue and most of it is not good. We tell ourselves things that we would never allow another person to say. We make up stories about ourselves that destroy our self-confidence and our potential as happy, healthy, loving, successful people. Emmett Fox says that an affirmation is a blueprint for the subconscious.

Émile Coué was a French psychologist and pharmacist born in 1857 who discovered the placebo effect. He noticed that when he praised the efficacy of a medication to customers, they got better than those customers who did not get the positive report about the medication. He urged clients to repeat this sentence twenty times in the morning and evening in a monotonous voice while sitting in a relaxed position "Every day, in every way, I am becoming better and better."

> "Every day, in every way, I'm getting better and better."
> — Émile Coué (1857–1926)

Guidelines for Writing Affirmations

- Positive self-statement—avoid using a negative word, you can't see the absence of something. What often happens when someone says "Don't trip on the steps?" You trip. Make it positive—I easily and safely walk down steps.
- Personal pronoun—Start with "I," you are talking about you.
- Present Tense—Now is when you want this to happen not tomorrow.

> "An affirmation is a blueprint for the subconscious."
> — Emmett Fox

Module 5 — Achieving Your 90-day Goals

Examples of Affirmations

I am happy, joyous, and free.
I am a loving, spiritual, and sober woman.
I put only what is healthy into my body.
I am confident.
I see opportunity everywhere.
I am enough, I have enough, I do enough.
I live in a world of abundance.
I attract all that is good in my life.

Measure Progress

Feedback improves performance and the best type of feedback gives you knowledge of results; it tells you whether you are winning or losing, whether you are getting closer to your goal or further away from your goal. It lets you know if you need to revise your actions.

Status: Red/ Yellow/ Green — I use green for on track, yellow for started or caution, and red for not yet started or in trouble.

Daily Check Sheet — Use this sheet on a daily basis to track what you accomplish each day. I use this for strength training and write how many reps I complete and how many sets.

Time — Track how much time you spend on a task daily, weekly, monthly.

Money — Track amount earned, saved, donated.

Daily Check Sheet

Goal/ Activity	1	2	3	4	5	6	7	8	9	10	11	12	13	14	15	16	17	18	19	20	21	22	23	24	25	26	27	28	29	30	31

Strategies to Help You Achieve Your Goals

Go from Big Picture to Today

Align your long-term goals with your vision and break down your goals into easy action steps by going from macro to micro. We create a vision by widening the lens and taking into account every possibility. We accomplish our goals by gradually shortening the time frame from years, to annual goals, 90-day goals, monthly goals, and weekly tasks until we are accomplishing the required action steps today. The diagram on the next page shows how we move from broad to specific.

An Example

Here is an example of how we could go about moving towards our vision of travelling all over the world.

```
Vision
5-10 Year Goals
Annual Goals
90 Day Goals
Monthly Goals
Weekly Tasks
Today's Action Steps
```

Vision

Travel all over the world, enjoying time with fellow travelers, learning about the history and culture of each area I visit.

5-year goals

Save $80,00 for two people to go to Europe for two weeks. Save $1,600 per year and $133 per month. Determine what countries and cities to visit.

12–18-month goals before trip

Make hotel reservations. Get a passport. Get airline tickets.
Visit Switzerland — Bern and Zurich, Germany — Duesseldorf, France — Paris.

90-day goals before trip

Rent car. Save $400 per quarter. Contact people I want to see in Europe and set up time to meet. Get someone to take care of the dog, water plants, and take in mail. Take vacation days. Identify museums and churches and other cultural historic sites.

Module 5 — Achieving Your 90-day Goals

Monthly goals

Save $133 per month. Save $31 per week.

Today's Action Steps (week before trip)

Make sure I have enough medication.

Share itinerary with family and close friends.

Start packing.

Decide how to get to the airport.

Leave key for person taking care of dog and house.

Create Desire for the Goal

Keep the goal in front of you in words or better yet a picture. Imagine yourself in possession of your goal with all the associated positive feelings. Identify all the benefits of the goal. Relate your goal to your values and mission. Pray "for this or something better."

> *"Focus more on your desire than on your doubt, and the dream will take care of itself."*
>
> *— Mark Twain*

Build Enthusiasm for the Journey

Ignite the flame of enthusiasm by remembering why you set this goal. Enjoy the journey. Know that you have released your desire into the universe and your goal is already being made manifest.

Build Belief that You Can Achieve the Goal

Envision yourself in possession of your goal. This mental practice builds belief. Measure your progress. Each step brings you a little closer.

Strengthen Your Commitment to Your Goals

Write down your goals and sign your commitment.

> "... the moment one definitely commits oneself, then providence moves too. All sorts of things occur to help one that would never otherwise have occurred. A whole stream of events issues from the decision, raising in one's favor all manner of unforeseen incidents and meetings and material assistance, which no man could have dreamt would have come his way.
>
> Whatever you think you can do or believe you can do, begin it. Action has magic, grace, and power in it."
>
> **— W.H. Murray**

The Scottish Explorer W.H. (William Hutchison) Murray taken from his book the Scottish Himalayan Experience

Story — Ellen Burton

Introduction to Ellen Burton

Ellen is the kind of person that makes you feel better about yourself. She walks into a room and instantly the mood elevator ascends; the mood is lighter and people are happier. I trust Ellen. After all, she was the first babysitter for our daughter.

> *"Nothing great was ever achieved without enthusiasm."*
>
> — Henry David Thoreau

Ellen Burton

Ellen Burton is my friend and a woman who took an ember of a dream, fanned it, and fed it into a blazing fire within; she became unstoppable!

In 1985, Ellen is working at the university in a dysfunctional sports medicine department. In an effort to improve the culture and reduce conflict, the department manager brings in a skilled facilitator to provide training in conflict management and communications. Ellen is mesmerized by the skills of the expert facilitator and decides that she wants to be a motivational speaker and adult learning trainer. On a quest to learn more, she seeks out Marianne Williamson and other motivational speakers, listens to their messages and reads their books; this empowers Ellen and frees her from limiting thoughts she didn't know she had.

In 1996, Ellen sees Maya Angelo at the Allstate Arena in Chicago and is amazed that the sports arena is filled to capacity. Ellen's father was a football coach for a Big Ten University and sports doubled as the family's religion. Her past and future seem to converge in a powerful way, and Ellen then knows what she is destined to do with her life. Her mission is to bring healing to the business community. She trains and becomes certified as a Personal and Professional Coach.

Ellen takes every opportunity to teach and speak. She attends events with Marianne Williamson, Oprah Winfrey, Lou Holtz, Zig Ziegler, and T.D. Jakes, watches TED talks and listens to the recordings of Martin Luther King. She is feeding the flames of enthusiasm! She is on fire!

Ellen is making six figures in pharmaceutical sales but it is no longer a challenge. Her work is not fulfilling.

Life's difficulties reveal themselves and Ellen forgets her dream, doesn't think it will happen, and becomes dejected and depressed; she can't see that God has a plan. Ellen asks for help, talks with her coach, and relies on God. She makes a 12-month plan with her coach to leave her high paying job and launch her own coaching and training business.

Ellen gets a part-time contract position at the Great Lakes Naval Station teaching young sailors in the computer learning center and participates in giving the orientation for sailors just out of bootcamp. Most presenters spent their 10-minute allotment reading a description of their department, yet Ellen intuitively knows to give a motivational presentation and has her audience laughing and cheering. Eventually, her time ends with a standing ovation from exhausted 18- and 19-year-olds. She realizes that she is doing it!! She is living her dream!

In places along her journey, self-doubt and exhaustion kick in. Fear of financial insecurity and not believing she is up to the task bog her down and she pushes away her dream. But it will not be ignored, it is down deep but stirring. Ellen knows her mission and is driven to be of service. She reaches out, she calls positive friends and colleagues, exercises her body, sleeps, renews her spirit, prays, and keeps on taking the steps necessary to manifest her dreams. She bears witness, sees that she is on the right path, and her faith grows.

Ellen begins to speak her vision out loud to others. She envisions a lifestyle where she is an internationally acclaimed author, lecturer, and motivational speaker. She creates vision boards and her enthusiasm grows.

She learns to constantly counter self-doubt and process discouraging events in the world with positive affirmations and strives to maintain her physical, spiritual, and mental health. She sees friends and associates accomplish the "impossible" and takes this as a message that she too can realize her dreams.

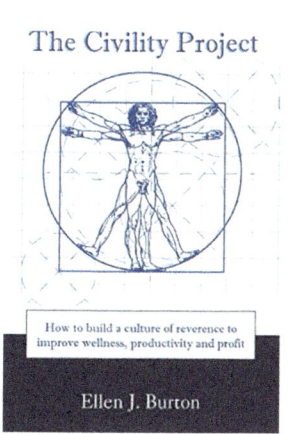

Today, 25 years in her own business, Ellen is in the zone; she is an inspirational leader, a nationally acclaimed motivational speaker, and a catalyst for change. She coaches executives and small business owners and facilitates women's leadership groups. She has published her book, *The Civility Project: How to build a culture of reverence to improve wellness, productivity and profit*,[28] and has launched The Civility Project to support organizations in building a culture of reverence with improved collaboration and engagement, leading to increased productivity. Ellen documents the tremendous costs to businesses of incivility and bullying. She urges both leaders and employees to assess their organizational culture and themselves in terms of their civility and compassion, to build a foundation of values and behavioral expectations, and to provide a structure of accountability to reinforce the expectations throughout the employee lifecycle from orientation to end of employment. Ellen stresses the importance of self-care, gratitude, and self-love as a path to loving others and treating them with respect.

Ellen no longer feels the need to prove herself. She knows what she excels at and is grateful to be able to use her gifts. Ellen encourages anyone who feels a spark of inspiration to follow your dream. She is more than 30 years sober, has a sponsor, works the steps, and practices a spiritual life. She speaks with authority and enthusiasm. According to the Online Etymology Dictionary, enthusiasm comes from the Greek word entheos that means "in God," divinely inspired. Ellen shines with God's love and believes that God, hope, and love are available to everyone — for free! She is happily and gratefully living a life beyond her wildest dreams!

Discussion

How did you feel about this story? What resonated with you? What did you learn about how this person created and implemented her vision? What could you apply?

Feelings	Thoughts that resonated with You
Action you will take	

> "Your heart's desire is the voice of God, and that voice must be obeyed sooner or later."
>
> — Emmet Fox

Developing a Habit of Planning — Daily, Weekly, Monthly

Bring your long-term dreams and goals into today by planning daily, weekly, and monthly. This is good time management, an essential skill to realize your dreams. Modify the following lists so that it works for you and then just do it!

Daily Planning

- Identify people to contact by phone or text.
- Schedule phone call time.
- Transfer tasks unfinished from yesterday to task list
- Review monthly goals.
- Review weekly goals.
- Add other tasks that need to be done.
- Read affirmations.
- Practice visualizing goals.
- Group similar activities like phone calls, letter writing, texting to avoid disrupting yourself every time you change activities.
- Prioritize tasks.

Weekly Planning

- Review accomplishments week before and update charts and graphs.
- Review monthly goals.
- Determine whether on track.
- Schedule letter writing time.
- Schedule personal learning time.
- Set weekly goals.
- Prioritize goals.
- Schedule time.

Monthly Planning

- Review annual goals and determine whether on track.
- Review last month's goals.
- Specify in quantitative terms, goals for at least the top three priority areas.
- Write down all other monthly goals by project or area of life.
- Prioritize your goals.
- Schedule weekly and daily planning time.
- Highlight time to work on at least top two priorities.
- Schedule time to work on long range projects.
- Review birthdays and other special occasions for upcoming month. List how you intend to honor those occasions and schedule time to purchase cards or presents.

What does the Research Say?

Research in goal setting has proved that specific goals produce specific results.[29] Numerous studies found a positive correlation between goal setting and performance.[30] Specific difficult goals produce higher performance than "do-your-best" goals.[31] When you focus on your vision and values, your motivation to achieve long-term goals increases, and your goals have meaning.[32]

Action Steps

Directions: check each circle when completed:

1. Review your goals and determine what you will accomplish in the next 90 days. ◯
2. Write three affirmations to help you accomplish your priority goals. Post it in a place where you will see it and read it daily. ◯
3. Track your goals daily. ◯
4. Envision yourself already having realized your goals while praying this or something better to allow room for greater things. Develop a daily 2-minute practice to visualize an important goal as though it has already happened. ◯
5. Insert daily, weekly and monthly planning into your calendar. Plan for the upcoming month, week, and day. ◯

Reflections

1. Journal on the role that intuition has played in your life and identify ways to increase it. ◯
2. Journal on the obstacles to achieving your goals. If this is what you really want, why don't you have it already? ◯
3. Practice spiritual automatic writing to ask and get answers to your questions. ◯
4. Journal on the visualization you created for your important goal.

Module 6

Travel Light

Objectives

At the end of this module, you will be able to:
- Decide what to take and what to leave behind so that you can travel light
- Describe the importance of letting go
- Identify thoughts, attitudes, beliefs, and habits that no longer serve you
- Create space for new blessings, ideas, and beliefs

Introduction

We all have baggage and with our arms, heads, hearts, and souls filled with this waste; it is impossible to embrace a future filled with light, love, and all good things. You have a suitcase in each hand; a dear friend who you have not seen in some time comes toward you. You let go of the bags and open your arms wide. My hope is that during this section you will decide what you can leave behind, let go of what is not in your power to change, and create space to embrace new blessings, ideas, and beliefs.

Celebration and Review

Here we are at Module 6. You have done good work! You have traveled to the future and seen the possibilities, listed dreams, set goals, and focused on what you need to do in the next 90 days. Your tool kit is growing and you are now using affirmations to build belief and are tracking your progress. Congratulations! We saw in Teri's story how God uses obstacles and difficulties to create changes and opportunities that we would not have thought possible. Ellen's story shows the power of enthusiasm and the importance of modeling ourselves after the people we admire.

> *"Travel light, live light, spread the light, be the light."*
>
> *— Harbhajan Singh Yogi*

Story — Melinda

Introduction to Melinda

I started a business called Training Dynamics when I was 27 years old. My goal was to identify prospective customers and call ten of them per day. Out of this, I would obtain 2-3 appointments to present the opportunity in person. I found prospects through the Chamber of Commerce directory, regional business news, and sometimes by just walking around. Walking down the main street in town, I came upon a store that had the door open and laughter emanating from inside. I stepped in and asked to speak to the manager and that is how I met Melinda.

Melinda

Sometimes circumstances force us to let go and rely on God. At 21 years old, Melinda was the manager of a store and when I made a sales presentation to her, I was struck by her enthusiastic, positive, bubbly personality. She and several of the people who worked with her enrolled in the Motivational Management course that I was teaching. Several years later, I got to meet her future husband James, an architect, when the two of them attended a retreat with me in the Helderberg Mountains. They were a positive couple with so much love and potential.

Melinda grew up in a household with many uncertainties. She dreamed of spending life with a very special husband... a sort of "knight in shining armor." She dreamed of feeling safe, secure, and unconditionally loved. At first, she thought that James was the fulfillment of that dream, but later learned that James partially fulfilled that, and ultimately it was Jesus who gave her the safety and unconditional love she was craving as a child. She dreamed that they would have children with happy childhoods filled with lots of nice memories and feelings of unconditional love.

Module 6 — Travel Light

Now married and with two little girls, the unthinkable happened: James was diagnosed with leukemia and would need a bone marrow transplant. They had to travel across the country to the Fred Hutchinson Cancer Research Center in Seattle, Washington for a procedure that could take anywhere from 3-18 months. Even amidst this challenging time, Melinda says that they had the privilege of seeing God's mighty hand at work every step of the way and felt a real peace when their circumstances would suggest otherwise. They prayed to find a house in Seattle overlooking water with a safe place for their girls. God led them to a beautiful $750,000 house on Mercer Island overlooking Lake Washington. The house had a 30 x 50-foot deck fenced in with mesh all around it so Jaime and Ashley could run around and not fall. Not only that, they also had a view of the city of Seattle so they could see "where daddy was staying." A member of the church they attended offered the house to them.

For Melinda, it was a peaceful setting, high on that hill overlooking the water with many pine trees that comforted her, and at night they could sit on the couch in the living room and see the cars drive over the floating bridge (it looked like a long pearl necklace draped over a piece of black velvet) behind the beautiful city skyline. Next to her on the couch, her best friend and kids ... who could ask for anything more?

One of Melinda's wildest dreams was to meet Amy Grant, the Country/Western Christian singer. "Her music really touched my heart when James was very ill, and I had such a strong desire to meet her and ask her if she would pray for James. Just by "coincidence" (As you know, I call them God-incidences!) while we were clear across the country in Seattle, WA during James' bone marrow transplant at Fred Hutchinson... there was an Amy Grant concert. My father sent one of my closest friends, Carol, and me the money to go. After the concert, we were riding home and I saw a bus leaving the concert. I thought, Amy Grant is probably on the bus, so we followed the bus down the highway and right off the same exit. I started to flash my headlights and lo and behold the bus pulled over and a gentleman got off (I assume it was her agent). When he asked what I wanted I simply told him I'd like to please speak with Amy Grant. As he was telling me I couldn't, I see these cowboy boots walk off the bus and it's her. She smiled and said she'd speak with me.

"What a wonderful person she was. I told her all about James and she told me she and the band would be happy to pray for him and she hugged me. Another gentleman who had also pulled over with a photo of Amy Grant (to get autographed for himself) heard James' story and gave her the photo to autograph for James. It was his birthday ... August 30, 1991."

About 6-7 months later, two days after James died, I was getting out of the shower when Carol told me the phone was for me. I said I didn't want to talk to anyone ... turns out it was Amy Grant's secretary—Amy had just called her (from Europe where she was on tour) and asked her if she would call me to find out how James was doing."

The girls were told that Daddy is in Heaven building a house for them.

Melinda remarried and is living the life she envisioned. Her daughters feel secure and loved. She has had the pleasure of introducing Amy Grant to her children—backstage at a concert in Albany at the Palace Theatre.

Discussion

How did you feel about this story? What with you? What did you learn about how this person created and implemented her vision? What could you apply?

Feelings	Thoughts that resonated with you
Action you will take	

> *"If you wish to travel far and fast, travel light. Take off all your envies, jealousies, unforgiveness, selfishness and fears."*
>
> *— Cesare Pavese*

Our Thoughts Affect Us Physically

Let's try an experiment. Close your eyes and extend both arms in front of you, hands facing up. Imagine that your left hand has a book, two books, three books on top. Imagine that your right hand has a string around it holding a cluster of helium filled balloons. Now look at your arms. If you are like most people, your left arm will be lower, weighted down while your right arm is lifted.

Module 6 — Travel Light

This demonstrates that our mind does not know the difference between what we see in our mind and what is physically occurring.

Stories We Tell Ourselves

Some of our thoughts are simply stories we make up and tell ourselves repeatedly. I tell myself that I am forgetful (especially with names), a klutz, and a poor public speaker. The more I tell myself that story, the more I believe it and act accordingly. We see pictures of others detailing their successes, their fun times, photos of family and friends. We see their wonderful lives and compare our insides to their outsides. We may tell ourselves that we don't measure up. We are not successes. Or, we see our friends' successes and inwardly cheer for them. You are glad that good things are happening for them. You feel grateful.

When I tell myself a negative story that isn't true, I draw closer to that belief. I look for things that will agree with that belief. I start feeling worse about myself.

What stories do you tell yourself? A recurrent theme among the people I have worked with is feeling not good enough. As an example, let's look at stories we tell ourselves about not being good enough versus being good enough.

"I am not good enough" Versus "I am good enough"

Let's brainstorm thoughts and feelings for each of the two sentences below.

I am not good enough.	I am good enough.

Identifying What to Leave Behind

I have a room where I have put my deceased mother's things along with my grown daughters' artworks, grades, photos, and clothes. It contains my dad's bowling scores carefully recorded in a notebook from 1953 until 2015 and a book of his poetry. Photos in frames, some broken, some not. I go in there sometimes and find a memory to enjoy. Along the way, I get distracted and overwhelmed. There is too much here in a cluttered mess. When I try to pick out the good, it gets tangled with something

I don't need. I am afraid to throw out something I might want or need later. Is it disrespectful to throw away the book containing the signatures of those who attended my grandfather's funeral? No, it does not give me joy. I have heard that I should pick up each object and ask whether it brings me joy. If not, dispose of it.

In the same way, my mind is sometimes cluttered. It contains hurts and resentments that replay on an endless loop: old messages about what is possible or not possible or how I need to be nice all the time, fears that hold me back, worries that keep me up at night about things that will never happen.

I am going on a trip to the Adirondacks. This requires careful planning because we will not be near any stores and we will be entertaining our extended family. My husband has ordered some of the food we will need. I have packed the coffee and will bring my own Nespresso machine as a backup. We have bug spray and sunscreen lotion. We will buy refrigerated and frozen items as we get closer. Sadly, I will be bringing myself with my fears, anxieties, and wants. I would love to clear out some space so that I can enjoy the moment, bring love, and experience the miracles.

I would like to:

> Move from self-seeking to seeking the will of my higher power.
>
> Transform my hurts from producing resentments to producing love.
>
> Move from self-serving relationships to relationships that serve God.
>
> Move ambitions from serving self to serving God.
>
> Move my relationship with money and possessions from ownership to stewardship.
>
> Transform fears to faith.
>
> Move from self-centered to God-centered.
>
> Transform my anxieties from producing self-protection to embracing God's loving protection.
>
> Move from self-talk that finds the holes in me to self-talk that sees my wholeness.

The Prayer of St. Francis describes this desire to be transformed and spirit-filled.

Prayer of St. Francis

Lord, make me an instrument of your peace,
Where there is hatred, let me sow love;
where there is injury, pardon;
where there is doubt, faith;
where there is despair, hope;
where there is darkness, light;
where there is sadness, joy;
Grant that I may not so much seek to be consoled as to console;
to be understood as to understand;
to be loved as to love.
For it is in giving that we receive;
it is in pardoning that we are pardoned;
and it is in dying that we are born to eternal life.

Through the grace of God, I only had to take two time-outs during my vacation. I was able to stay in the moment and be present for my family; I enjoyed the time with each person. What a gift!

Habits, Attitudes, and Beliefs that No Longer Serve You

To embrace your future self and all the fabulous events that will come to pass in your life, you need to let go of those things that are in the way. Prayerfully make a list of the habits, attitudes, and beliefs that no longer serve you so that you can make room for love and peace. Use your notebook for this. You could make separate lists for resentments, fears, habits, relationships, money and possessions, anxieties, etc. This is a lifelong process. In Step 6 of *The 12 Steps of Alcoholics Anonymous*, we decided that we "were entirely ready to have God remove all these defects of character," and Step 7: we "humbly asked Him to remove our shortcomings." Our goal is to "gain a vision of humility as the avenue to true freedom of the human spirit." Fully enter into the belief that your vision is a current fact and act as if it is true.

Forgiveness

When I have a resentment, the movie inside my head plays repeatedly, making me feel worse and worse. It is like taking poison and expecting the other person to die. It is only hurting me. Forgiveness is the only way out. I forgive to restore my connection to the other person and God. It is a spiritual process. I pray for the other person; I pray that they will be happy, joyous, and free.

With prayer, forgive yourself for any perceived wrongdoing or imperfection. Envision how you would like the relationship to be and what you are feeling about the relationship.

Some years ago, when I had just started my job with an automotive supplier in Michigan, I was invited by the Vice President of Manufacturing to meet with his Plant Managers at a two-day offsite meeting in Delaware. I was asked to talk to more than forty men about a learning needs assessment I had completed for the business. The needs assessment was based on interviews with senior leaders of each business and a sample of plant managers. They were asked to identify key gaps in business results and job performance. I shared the priority learning needs with the group. The VP stood up and said, "I question your data. I don't believe what you say is true." I felt attacked and was embarrassed. I wished that I could have disappeared. I was so angry at him for belittling me in front of people I had just met. The next morning, I saw the VP alone at breakfast and I told him that I felt attacked. He did not apologize; he invited me to "process the event." I had a resentment for a long time. I prayed for him and I prayed for the relationship. I envisioned a positive relationship with this man; he would be my best supporter. We would work side by side, a relationship of mutual respect. I prayed for this or something better. I started to notice that the fear was gone, and I was able to interact with him as an adult; one person interacting with another. I reflected on my vision as he and I enjoyed dinner on the fast train from Cologne, Germany to Paris, France. We were going to implement a leadership training program for business leaders in France. He was now my manager and my best supporter.

I am reminded of the four paradoxes of recovery: our ego died so we could live; we let go to have power; we suffered to get well; and we surrendered to win!

Beliefs

Beliefs are so powerful they can enable us to do what no one else has been able to do. Beliefs enabled Roger Bannister to break the 4-minute mile and enabled others to believe that they too could run a mile faster than 4 minutes. Belief enabled me to get a job interview that had been cancelled; I believed so strongly that this was "my job" that I called the hiring manager rather than accept what was. Kathryn knew she was an interior designer, left her administrative job, sold her house, and enrolled in design school in New York City.

The Room

I set a goal to clear out the little room in my house where all the memories are stored. My sister has left for Mexico and has given me two boxes of childhood photos. I put these in the room along with a box of silver plates, a silver teapot, and other silver objects. I have now entered the closet with a tiny door with crawl space. My husband had lovingly stored at least twenty boxes from our move in 2007. I uncover my master's thesis from the 1980's with all the research on goal setting and strategic planning, binders of training programs I had developed, research studies conducted with my mentor on Teacher Centers in New York State, and marketing studies for community colleges. I find a binder on my goals accomplished with letters and awards I had forgotten ever receiving.

I have been trying to uncover my unconscious beliefs by identifying my childhood perceptions of my parents. My dad had a sensitive side; he would choke up while reading a human-interest story in the paper, but he was critical, did not otherwise express his feelings, and was often unavailable. I wanted acknowledgement of my deepest self and, after not finding it, addressed it with anger, rebellion, drinking, and, finally, just shutting down and disappearing. In this crawl space, I now realize that I had prevented myself from getting this acknowledgement by being invisible. If I am not taking up any space, I can't be hurt. "Coincidentally," as I am working through the origin of my beliefs from my father, I find that, in the binder of goals accomplished, there are two poems written by my dad. He does get me. He does acknowledge me.

On my 18th birthday, I found one such poem on my desk.

Dear Linda

The years slip by, too fast it seems,
The past replaces future's dreams.
If we could each go back in time,
We'd falter less, we'd speed the climb.

Today you've reached a magic place,
A step in life, —time won't erase.
The magic of youth's milestone day.
Eighteen years—what more to say!!

You've demonstrated special gifts;
God must have worked 12-hour shifts.
He's given you a bright warm smile;
A temper too, but lots of style;
Self-discipline and dedication
Moving you towards education.
But most of all a loving heart
That's made you do more than your part.

Keep reaching out and helping others,
Even irritants—like brothers!
Just rush ahead and do your best;
Your faith and God will do the rest.
Enjoy the good, endure the bad,
For all your talents please be glad.

I've watched you grow; I know you well
You're more to me than words can tell!!
So, when your problems get you down,
And life's bright green, seems more like brown.
Remember though the world seems shrill
I love you now and always will.

Happy Birthday!!

Dad

I can let go of the belief that I was not acknowledged for being who I am. I was committed to believing many falsehoods I told myself. The obstacle in my way was me and my beliefs. What if I just accepted myself and brought my whole self wherever I go? I don't need to be critical of myself, and I don't need to attract people who are critical of me. I can believe that I *am* worthy of getting paid for my time. I accept my life exactly as it is right now.

> *"Receive with simplicity everything that happens to you."*
>
> **— Rashi**

Guided Imagery — The Park Bench

Introduction to Guided Imagery

This powerful guided imagery will enable you to let go of those thoughts, feelings, and resentments that are holding you back.

The Park Bench

Sit in a comfortable position with your feet on the ground and your shoulders back. Let's begin by taking a deep breath. Breathe in love and kindness. Breathe out suffering. Take another slow, slow deep breath. Breathe in peace. Let the air out slowly. Breathe out any disturbances. Take another deep breath, allowing yourself to become more and more relaxed. Relax your face, neck, shoulders, and arms. Let your arms feel very heavy. Let your back relax. Let the muscles in your abdomen and hips become more and more relaxed. Let your legs and feet relax. You are alert but your body feels very heavy and relaxed. Let your attention come to your heart. Breathe into your heart, experience love and mercy. Say to yourself—I am willing to let go of pain and suffering. I am ready to enter my true nature as a loving, peaceful, kind soul. I am loving, peaceful, and kind.

Imagine you are starting out on your journey to create an amazing, extraordinary future. You have two bags of luggage. They are big and heavy. Pick them up and notice how heavy they are. In your right hand, you are carrying all the negative experiences with the regrets, hurts, grudges, and resentments of the past. Take a moment to reflect on the items you are carrying from the past... Know that the past cannot be changed, but we can make peace with the past, make amends to those we have hurt, learn from our mistakes, and do our best going forward. In your left hand, you are carrying the fears and worries about tomorrow... Take a moment to reflect on what you are afraid of... your fears about the future... your worries.... You know that tomorrow will come and that most of our worries and fears about the future never come to pass... These bags are very, very heavy. You don't need them. You only have this moment. Imagine putting those bags down and seeing yourself moving along the path freely... You now have more space to fill with love and light.

See yourself in a beautiful, safe place in a secluded wood. Here you can feel the love and beauty in the world. Follow the path. Come to an open space with a bench. Sit down on the bench. Imagine a puppy is on your lap. Notice how tender you are towards this puppy. Your heart softens and opens. This love is natural for you. If this puppy did something to disturb you, you would forgive. Forgiveness is your natural state. You would not take it personally. You would know it is not about you. In your loving state you may be wondering, what could they have done to hurt me?

Now imagine that someone you need to forgive comes and sits on the bench. What this person did was not right, however it is in the past. You choose to be happy and this resentment gets in the way. Imagine looking into their eyes while letting your heart open. Say some words of forgiveness... Wish them love, peace, happiness... Hear what the other person says in return... Notice how the love of God surrounds you both and you are connected. You are blessed with peace and a stronger connection to God.

The person disappears.

You notice that a hand mirror is on the bench and you pick it up. Look into your eyes. You know that you do enough, you have enough, and you are enough. Still, you may need to forgive yourself for something. Perhaps you have expected too much. Look upon yourself with an open heart as you did a kitten or baby. Take some moments and say what you need to forgive yourself... Let the ocean of compassion wash over you. Let your whole body soften into this loving kindness embracing you. Let yourself be healed in forgiveness and love. See the light from your higher power embracing you, filling your heart with light and joy. See yourself as you truly are. Let this love and light extend to someone you love, entering their heart, filling them with love and compassion and healing. Extend this love to your family... your community... your world... until everyone is connected in love and light filled with compassion, kindness, and grace.

It is time to return to this room. Know that you can return to this loving connection and forgiveness whenever you wish. Take this love and compassion into your life. Become aware of my voice, the chair you are sitting on, feel your hands and your feet. Wiggle your fingers and toes. When you are ready, gently and gradually open your eyes. Return to this room. Jot down some notes about your experience.

Guided Imagery Reflections

Take a few moments to jot down any thoughts or feelings that occurred to you during this meditation. Did anything surprise you? How did you feel? What lies are you invested in?

Releasing Negative Emotions

Tapping (Emotional Freedom Technique)

We all have unresolved emotional issues that get in the way of living the life we desire. Emotional Freedom Technique (EFT), better known as "tapping," is an alternative healing treatment for physical pain and emotional distress. Tapping is the general process, and EFT refers to the specific type of tapping. It is a powerful method to reduce stress and anxiety, let go of negative emotions, and enable you to access your better self. The process provides the physical benefits of acupressure (from ancient Chinese medicine) by tapping on the endpoints of meridians in our bodies, and adds the emotional and cognitive benefits of modern psychotherapy.

Tapping regulates the nervous system, sends a calming signal to the brain, and strengthens the immune system. Cortisol, best known as the hormone that triggers the "fight or flight" syndrome with the rapid heartbeat, is the central focus of tapping. Research in 2012 by Dawson Church, Ph.D. showed that subjects who "tapped" for just one hour decreased cortisol levels by an average of 24 percent, and some decreased cortisol by up to 50 percent. The control group received talk therapy and the cortisol levels in that group decreased by 14 percent.[33]

To learn more about tapping go here: What Is Tapping And How Can I Start Using It? (thetappingsolution.com)

Steps for Tapping[34]

1. Identify an emotional or physical issue.
2. On a scale of 1–10, rate the intensity with 10 being in the highest level of distress or pain.
3. Create a set-up statement in which you acknowledge the issue and accept yourself exactly as you are. For example, "Even though I have this _____ (pain, anxiety, fear, etc.), I deeply and completely love and honor myself."
4. Follow the EFT Tapping sequence (continue with 3-5 rounds or more)
    a. Karate chop- tap with 4 fingers 5-6 times on the side (below your pinkie) of your other hand while repeating the set-up statement each time you tap.
    b. Eyebrow- tap with two fingers on one side of your face. Repeat the issue, the story you are telling yourself about the issue as you tap through each of the points in the first round.
    c. Under the eye
    d. Under the nose
    e. Chin
    f. Collarbone
    g. Under the arm
    h. Top of the head
5. Identify where you feel it in your body. Gradually, add more acceptance and the willingness to let it go. Add positive statements about yourself.
6. Recheck the intensity level 1-10.

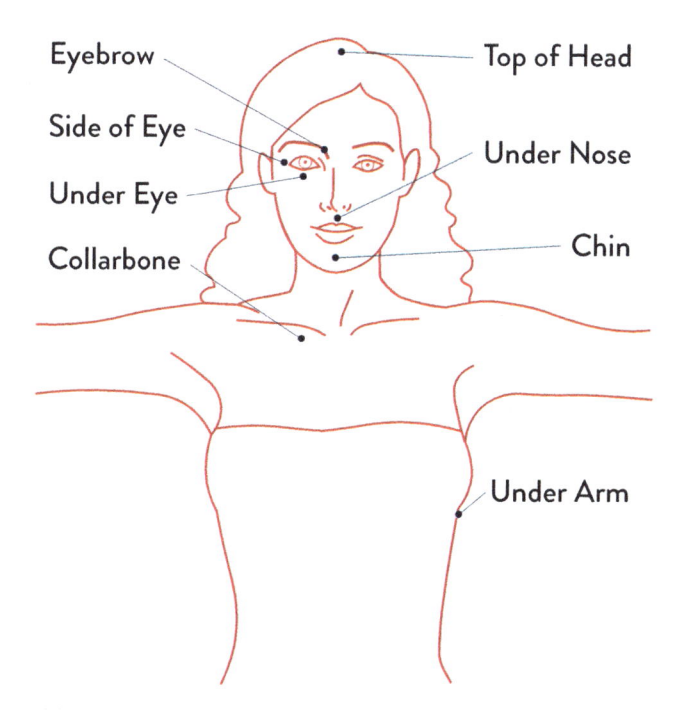

- Eyebrow
- Side of Eye
- Under Eye
- Collarbone
- Top of Head
- Under Nose
- Chin
- Under Arm

Over one hundred studies demonstrating the effectiveness of Clinical EFT have been published in peer reviewed journals. Participants in a four-day training for Clinical EFT received a series of pre and post physiological assessments. After the training, participants experienced a significant reduction in anxiety (-40%), depression (-35%), post traumatic stress disorder (-32%), pain (-57%), and cravings (-78%). Happiness significantly increased (+32%). Participants experienced physiological changes in lowered blood pressure, and decreased cortisol levels (- 37%).[35]

You can find many good resources for tapping, including the app called The Tapping Solution, where you will find a library of tapping for numerous symptoms. A study of more than 270,000 app uses showed a significant reduction in stress and anxiety following a session of tapping.[36] I recommend Nick Ortner's book *The Tapping Solution for Manifesting Your Greatest Self: 21 Days to Releasing Self-Doubt, Cultivating Inner Peace, and Creating a Life You Love*[37] and the Nick and Jessica Ortner's annual, free week-long tapping meditation series. Go to this website for more information: www.thetappingsolution.com.

Dawson Church has developed a meditation process that incorporates tapping and has enabled thousands of first-time meditators to learn meditation quickly. In his books *Mind to Matter*[38] and *Bliss Brain*[39], Dawson Church provides scientific evidence that tapping and meditation work.

Neurolinguistic Programming—Timeline

Dissociation

Think of a goal you would like to accomplish in the next 90 days. Imagine a timeline extending towards your goal. See all the tasks. Move the timeline away from you so that you are no longer part of the timeline. It is separate from you. You have dissociated yourself from it. See each task and notice that you are feeling neutral about it, decide how to handle each one. When you are working on a task and begin to feel overwhelmed, re-visit the timeline dissociated from you.

Shrinking

Imagine a timeline extending towards your goal. See all the tasks. Notice any obstacles. Shrink the obstacle. Shrink it more until you can step over it. In your mind, you have overcome the obstacle. When working on the goal and you start feeling overwhelmed due to an obstacle, remember: shrink it down.

Guided Imagery — Embracing Wholeness and Inviting the Next Chapter

Introduction to Embracing Wholeness Guided Imagery

You are now ready to embrace your wholeness and invite the next chapter of your life. Happy people express gratitude and help others. According to the [Yale Happiness Course](#)[40] taken by over 3 million people, they also get enough sleep. During this guided imagery, we will explore what it feels like to have a grateful, loving heart and being of service to others.

Embracing Wholeness Guided Imagery

Go to your special place where you feel safe to dream. Allow yourself to get comfortable and relax. This is your space, your time. Take a deep breath, breathing in light and joy. Release any remaining negative emotions. Center yourself in the power, love, and wisdom of God. Sink down deeply to your center, your soul. Know that you are a whole spiritual being filled with love and light, grateful for your life as it is. Let's count from 10 to 1 to enable us to become even more relaxed. 10, 9, 8, you are becoming more relaxed and your arms are feeling very heavy. 7, 6, allow your neck and face to relax, 5, your back and abdomen become more relaxed, 3, your legs feel heavy and deeply relaxed, 2, 1, you are alert yet relaxed and are ready to welcome guidance from your higher power. You are a powerful, loving person open to the miracles of life. With humility, you have moved from a focus on yourself toward others and toward God. Let God be God in you. See God in others.

Now that you have cleared out those things you no longer need, you are travelling lightly; you have more room to embrace your wholeness and the miracles of life. Anything is possible. Take a moment to invite the next chapter into your life. You could say to yourself, "I welcome an extraordinary spiritual life filled with joy to fulfill my highest purpose." You can use this magic wand if you like. Allow whatever thoughts, feelings, or pictures to emerge... Whatever you experience is right for you. I will pause for a few moments... See yourself in possession of your goals, feeling at peace, loving, kind, confident, and powerful. You wear life like a loose garment. You have, with grace, transformed all negatives into positives. Imagine this new chapter in vivid color and strong positive emotions. Envision yourself happy, joyous, and free... Take some moments to thoroughly enjoy this next chapter.

See the path towards this life in front of you. The steps are clear; you will be guided. If an obstacle appears, shrink it and step over it. You are strong and resilient! Your relationships serve your higher power and others. Your ambitions are spiritual. You are a good steward of your money and possessions. Through God's grace, you have gained a vision of humility as the avenue to true freedom of your human spirit. See how you are in service to God and others.

Know that you can return to this space anytime. When you are ready, it is time to return to this room. Imagine climbing up the steps to the here and now. 1, 2, 3, become more alert, 4, 5, 6, hear my voice, feel the chair...7, 8, 9... wiggle your fingers and toes, 10, gently and gradually open your eyes.

Guided Imagery Reflections

Take a few moments to jot down any thoughts or feelings that occurred to you during this meditation. Did anything surprise you? How did you feel? How can you be of service to God and others?

Guided Imagery — Wearing Life Like a Loose Garment

Introduction to Guided Imagery

In the previous guided imagery, you imagined wearing life like a loose garment. This guided imagery will give you an opportunity to imagine practicing mindfulness.

Wearing Life Like a Loose Garment

Go to your special, sacred place where you can feel relaxed and connected to your higher power, the place where you feel at your best... Take a deep breath in and slowly let it out. Take another deep breath and breathe in peace... feel that peace spread throughout your body... Take another deep breath... Notice how it feels to take in fresh air... Put your hand on your heart and allow it to open with love... Take another deep breath, breathing in love. Let the love spread throughout your body. Once more, breathe in love and peace and breathe out all negative thoughts. Notice how easy it is to breathe out. Allow every muscle to relax deeply. Allow your mind to stay alert and in the moment without judgement.

Think about yesterday and how you moved through the day. See yourself doing. Notice any tightness in your body or negative thoughts that arise. On a scale of 1–10, identify your level of stress with 10 being the worst. How did you feel about yourself?

With this magic wand, change into loose garments. Let's remember that we are spiritual beings rather than human "doings"... Imagine how it would feel to wear life like a loose garment... Let's imagine a typical household chore. Imagine removing clothes from the dryer and folding the clothes. Feel your mind, body, and spirit connected as one. You are one with God. Pray. Feel grateful and in the flow. Rest in God's love. Now pick up a shirt and feel the warmth from the drying. Stay in the moment as you fold the shirt, feeling God's love. One by one, fold each item joyfully, lovingly, and meditatively. Fold each item prayerfully and with gratitude. When you have completed the task, pause. Allow yourself to feel good about what you have done. Celebrate!

On a scale of 1–10, identify your level of stress with 10 being the worst. How did you feel about yourself?

Think about some tasks for the week. Imagine starting and completing the first task in the same loving, joyful, and meditative way. See each step you will take ... Complete each task prayerfully and with gratitude. Life is easy, one moment at a time.

It is now time to return to this room. Become aware of the room and the chair you are sitting on. Move your body gently, starting with your fingers and toes ... When you are ready, gently and gradually open your eyes.

Guided Imagery Reflections

Take a few moments to jot down any thoughts or feelings that occurred to you during this meditation. Did anything surprise you? How did you feel?

What does the Research Say?

Guided imagery significantly reduces anxiety[41] in subjects who were diagnosed with either alcohol dependence or alcohol abuse. Alcohol, chemical, and behavioral addictions have been linked to stress, which guided imagery mitigates. People diagnosed with substance use disorder are more likely to have an anxiety disorder at three times the rate of the general population and are four times more likely to have depression.

Individualized guided imagery scripts were created for the study participants based on their spiritual, stressful, and neutral experiences. They rated the subjective intensity of spiritual connection and anxiety before and after listening to each guided imagery. Their subjective rating correlated to magnetic resonance imaging of their brain. When individuals experienced a strong spiritual connection, the parietal cortex was activated. The parietal cortex was suppressed when listening to the stressful guided imagery. [42]

Researchers found a pattern of neural networks associated with spiritual experiences recalled through guided imagery. This could have important implications for the prevention and treatment of behavior and substance abuse addictions. [43]

> *"I would like to travel light on this journey of life, to get rid of the encumbrances I acquire each day.... The most difficult thing to let go is myself, that self which, coddled and cozened, becomes smaller as it becomes heavier. I don't understand how and why I come to be only as I lose myself, but I know from long experience that this is so."*
>
> — Madeleine L'Engle

Action Steps

Directions: check each circle when completed:

1. List the habits and beliefs that no longer serve you. ○
2. Identify the stories you tell yourself that are not true. ○
3. Envision yourself being of service to God and others. Journal about what this looks like. ○
4. Practice affirmations and visualizations.. ○

Reflections

1. Practice spiritual writing to ask what habits and beliefs that no longer serve you. ○
2. Ask how you can make room for more joy. ○
3. Practice spiritual automatic writing to ask and get answers to your questions. ○
4. Envision the next chapter in your life and write it down. ○

Module 7

Overcoming Obstacles

Objectives

At the end of this module, you will be able to:

- Build your belief in yourself and your goals
- Identify types of obstacles
- Identify solutions to overcome each type of obstacle
- Focus on your desired result not the obstacle

> *"Believe in yourself and all that you are. Know that there is something inside you greater than any obstacle."*
>
> — *Christian Larson, Author of* The Great Within, *1907*

Introduction

As Christian Larson says, there is something inside of you greater than any obstacle! Most of our obstacles are in our minds. We will build your belief in yourself and in your goals. Let's take a look at the obstacles to your dreams and transcend them!

Celebration and Review

In our last session, you let go of some of the habits and beliefs that may be holding you back. You practiced forgiveness, embraced wholeness and welcomed the next chapter of your life. You are making progress in accomplishing your goals! You are being of service to your higher power and to others. Congratulations!

> *"When I dare to be powerful—to use my strength in the service of my vision—then it becomes less and less important whether I am afraid."*
>
> — Audre Lorde, Feminist, Civil Rights Activist and Poet

Belief in Yourself and Your Goals

Belief in Yourself and Your Goals

Believing in yourself and your ability to accomplish your goals is key to your success. Remember all the good you have done and all the successes you have had. Take just three minutes to list some of the successes you have had in your life.

Your Gifts and Talents

Everyone has gifts and talents they can contribute to the world. Think about what brings you joy and happiness.

Blocks

What are the blocks to your success? What limiting thoughts are preventing you from being the powerful, divine person you are? What is the downside to stepping into your power? Access the part of yourself that is resisting and ask it why it is blocking you from moving forward. See if you can negotiate a way forward.

I meditated on my goal to have a magnificent business enabling others to create a vision. I asked whether any part of me objects to the goal and if so to show me an image. My throat closed. It said I needed to relax and stop pushing. I asked if any other part of me objected to me taking my power and speaking up. A gnome-like creature zipped into sight and said that she objected. I asked why and she said that "you'll embarrass us."

Module 7 — Overcoming Obstacles

Identify Obstacles to Specific Goals

If this is what you really want, then why haven't you already achieved it? I ask myself this question and all the excuses and rationalizations pop up. I don't have enough time, I have too many things to do, I am afraid that someone will think less of me or not like me unless I do something else. I am not good at this, I don't have the skills... Write each one down in your notebook and identify how to deal with it.

Obstacles and Solutions

We often face many of the same obstacles. It is okay to recognize these obstacles, but don't give them power by focusing on them. Focus instead on the desired result. In 12 Step recovery programs, we say "work the program, not the problem." A problem is a great opportunity to refine your goal, vision, and plan.

> **Time**—We think we don't have enough time. We all have the same amount of time and we can choose how we allocate our time. Successful people focus on one task at a time.
>
> **Money**—We don't have enough money. Most goals don't require enormous amounts of money. We are all responsible for how we earn, invest, and spend our money.
>
> **Fear**—We are afraid to step out and seize a goal; what if we fail? What if we succeed? Replace fear with faith and love.
>
> **Too Many Goals**—We make demands on ourselves to accomplish too many goals at the same time. Evaluate your goals and the time you think it will take to reach them. Then, double the time and or cut the goals in half. Focus on your top three goals.
>
> **Lack of Action**—We want the result, but we don't take the necessary steps to succeed. Break down the steps needed to accomplish your goals.
>
> **Belief**—We don't believe we can accomplish the goal. We don't believe in ourselves. Affirm your success. Some people have difficulty remembering positive experiences. Both positive and negative experiences that are inconsistent with core beliefs tend to be ignored or minimized even if the experience enhances positive self-esteem.[44] Build belief by reliving a positive experience that counters a core negative belief. Use tapping to get rid of the harmful beliefs and tap in new beliefs.
>
> **Negative Automatic Thoughts**—We tend to tell ourselves things that we would not allow anyone else to say to us. Sometimes negative self-talk tells us we are

stupid, not competent, not loveable, or maybe not even deserving to be here. It can pop up out of the blue or they may be recurring thoughts. Usually, I just say "thank you for the information, now go away," and the thought subsides.

An exercise taken from the academic journal, Cognitive Behavioral Therapy, may be helpful. Examine the thought and the feelings it brings up. Identify any images or memories associated with the thought describing in detail what you hear, see, touch and smell. Identify what the image means. Identify the evidence for and against the thought with specific examples or memories. Then, we need to counter the negative thought with a more balanced thought such as "I am competent." By incorporating imagery into the thought, we address the negative automatic thought on an experiential and emotional level. Add a picture in your mind of a time when you felt competent and were competent. Make it as specific as possible. [45]

Distractions—Life happens, and other things get in the way. We momentarily lose sight of our dreams and goals and allow other things to get in the way. Visualize yourself in possession of your goals every day. Affirm they will be accomplished. Be grateful for the accomplishment of your goals in advance.

Age—We feel we are too young or too old. You are right where you are supposed to be! Use age to your advantage, whether it's the energy of youth or the wisdom of age.

Guided Imagery — Embracing the Life of Your Dreams

Introduction to Guided Imagery

This guided meditation will take you on a fanciful journey in your own personal space bubble. Your destination—embracing the life of your dreams!

Embracing the Life of Your Dreams

Your journey has begun. You need do nothing. Everything that you need is already here. Imagine...

A warm golden sun, a blue sky, a beautiful beach with white sand that seems to stretch forever...

A turquoise ocean with gentle waves... the sunlight dancing on the waves...

A blanket is spread out on the sand. A very comfortable lounge chair is available... Imagine yourself relaxing...

You have plenty of time. Use this time to begin letting go of any concerns or anxiety...

First, take a deep breath... and release it slowly. And then another... and release, letting go of all tension. Now, breathe normally and be aware of how you are feeling at this moment.

If you brought a great deal of stress with you, acknowledge its presence without criticism. When you are ready to release that tension, you will do so. Take one more deep breath, and then exhale any hurtful feelings, any anxieties or tensions, any negative attitudes, for they are of no use to you here.

If distracting thoughts come into your awareness, accept them and let them pass through your mind without judgement. If you hear any external noises, let them enable you to go deeper into this experience.

Imagine that any negative energy you brought with you is not needed for this journey and, if you want to, you can let the breeze carry it away. In this meditation, you will decide just how relaxed you want to be.

As much as you are able to do so, stay in the moment. Look at the ocean as if you have never seen it before.

Notice the colors.

Watch one wave and follow it with your attention from far in the distance...

Feel the sun against your body. Lie back on the blanket, or let the chair recline so that you can stretch out and feel the sun warming you, healing you.

Listen to the ocean and hear the crashing waves coming to the shore... Follow the sound of them to their last whispers on the sand. Is there a bird, perhaps a seagull in the distance? Listen...

Taste your lips and notice the subtle awareness of salt from the sea air. Take a deep breath and enjoy the cool, refreshing scent of the air.

Feel the sun — warm against your skin ... Think of the golden color of the sun and feel that warmth on your skin ... Breathe it into your lungs and let the healing, soothing energy of the sun fill your body and move all through you, into your shoulders and neck, up into your head, warming ... healing ... feel it moving into your arms ... hands ... fingertips ... into your back ... healing ... taking you deeper and deeper into relaxation ... making you feel good about yourself ... taking you deeper and deeper ... Feel the golden sun move through your hips and abdomen... down your thighs ... calves ...

ankles … down into your feet … you are completely relaxed and serene.

In the distance, you see a personal space bubble. It will take you on a magical journey … See the natural wonders of the world, the national parks, amazing beautiful waterfalls with crystal clear water … Giant redwoods in California … Majestic mountains … The desert with small towns with homes painted in bright colors… giant rivers with rushing rapids … See a world of abundance … See all the people you love and who love you … You can go anywhere and see anyone… there is enough for everyone … you have enough … Pick a spot and tell the bubble to land … Step out …

In the distance, you see a beautiful bridge. See the colors and design of the bridge as you approach more closely … This bridge is your bridge … This is a magical bridge … It will take you to the magical place where anything is possible… Walk towards the bridge

As you step on the bridge, you feel the magic of the place … the bridge will carry you to the future … 10 years into the future … the bridge may be short or long … you cross … walk through the fog … emerge through the fog … as you emerge, you notice something …

A being of light and love is standing there, holding out a beautifully wrapped box … the being communicates that the box contains all the gifts that you bring to the world … they are your spiritual gifts and talents … it is safe for you to take charge of your own life … the being encourages you to unwrap these gifts and show them to the world … remove the beautiful bow … remove the paper … open the box and see your gifts … take some moments to see yourself fully using your gifts … this is what you are meant to do … use your gifts … fully embrace all the goodness that is you. There are gifts that you bring to the world … they are unique to you … you are essential to the world … the being takes your hand and shows you moments of your past, of you using your gifts … the people in your life … the quality of your relationships … the being shows you the abundance in your life … the things you enjoy doing … your health and fitness … the things you have learned … your connection to your higher power … your contributions to others … your financial health and some of the ways you have enjoyed your earnings … travel… possessions … You see yourself fully embracing and living the life of your dreams … your home … your loved ones … your time together … your passion … take some moments to fully enjoy your life …

Guided Imagery Reflections

Take a few moments to jot down any thoughts or feelings that occurred to you during this meditation. Did anything surprise you? How did you feel? Did you see the being of light and love? What were the gifts?

> *"What separates an ordinary woman from an extraordinary woman? The belief that she is ordinary."*
>
> — *Jody Williams, 1997 Nobel Peace Prize Winner for her work on the International Campaign to Ban Landmines*

Identify the Obstacles to Living the Life of Your Dreams

Write down all the ways in which you limit your desires and creativity. How are you not doing what you want?

Guided Imagery — Learning from your Resistance

Introduction to Guided Imagery

As we advance in our journey, we often find that a part of us resists. This guided meditation will enable you to explore that resistance and see what you can do to overcome it. You will have the help of a special advisor.

Learning from your Resistance

Imagine yourself going to a special, peaceful inner place ... a place of great beauty, peacefulness, and safety. Look around and notice the beauty, the sounds, the smells ... Notice how good you feel to be here ... safe, comfortable, healing ... Find the most comfortable spot for you and settle in ... You feel safe and calm ... centered ...

Within you is your higher power—a place of all-knowing, all-loving and wisdom...

When you are ready, ask yourself if there is any part of you that is resisting your path of healing and growth ... You might ask about a specific goal. Does any part of you have any objections or concerns? ... Ask and quietly listen for a response ... let all your inner parts know that this is a place for healing and they are welcome to state their concerns ... all concerns will get a fair hearing ...

If all is quiet, and you sense there are no objections, invite your special advisor to appear and have a talk ... If there are any concerns or objections, invite that part to appear in your special place so that you can understand the concerns ...

Allow an image to form that represents this part of you. Notice what it looks like and what qualities it conveys ... notice any feelings that come up for you ...

Thank the image for coming to your awareness and invite it to be comfortable with you ... Allow it to share its concerns, in a way you can understand ... ask any questions you have... Thank it for giving you this information and accept the information whether you agree or not. Consider the information and ask, "if I could address your concerns, would you stop resisting?" Ask and let it answer. Ask for suggestions on how you could address its concerns and continue on your path of growth.

Consider each suggestion and imagine yourself carrying out the suggestion that feels the best to you... imagine this happening successfully ... there may even be ways this part of you can contribute to your healing and growth ...

If no suggestions are presented, ask your special advisor and this part of you to search together for creative solutions that will meet the needs... suggest meeting in 3-4 days to learn about the solutions... arrange a time to meet.

Ask whether there are any other concerns and repeat the process... Invite all parts of you to join in healing, to become whole, and to find ways to work together.

When finished for today... thank all parts of you... thank your special advisor... Imagine all the parts of you and your special advisor working together for your healing...

When you are ready, it is time to return... gently and gradually open your eyes.

Guided Imagery Reflections

Take a few moments to jot down any thoughts or feelings that occurred to you during this meditation. Did anything surprise you? How did you feel? What resistance did you tap into? Were you able to work out a way to overcome that resistance?

Guided Imagery — Breaking Through Obstacles

Introduction to Guided Imagery

This guided meditation will enable you to identify and break through obstacles. Take this magic wand with you.

Breaking Through Obstacles

Allow yourself to become more and more relaxed by whatever method works for you. You are walking along a path in a beautiful green meadow. You follow the path. Notice a series of flagstone steps leading down into a garden. You are starting from the 10th step and with each step you will become more relaxed … 9, 8, … 7, 6, 5 … 4, 3 … 2, 1 … Allow yourself to appreciate all the good, the beauty, the peace …

You come to a place in the path where you can see what appears to be a wall. The wall represents some obstacle that you are encountering in accomplishing your goals. See an image that represents the obstacle or hear a description … Whatever comes up for you is what you need to know … This journey is magical … you know that you will accomplish your goal. Continue on the path with strong belief in yourself and your goal … As you get closer to the wall—you realize that the wall is only tissue paper and all you need do is walk through.

Guided Imagery Reflections

Take a few moments to jot down any thoughts or feelings that occurred to you during this meditation. Did anything surprise you? How did you feel?

Gaining Focus with Priorities

In the third session, we identified priorities for your life. Now, we are going to focus in on the daily priorities that will enable you to accomplish your goals. Identify five priorities for each day. These priorities should be aligned with your values, mission, vision, and goals. Identify the five priorities that will bring you closer to your goals. Write this on a card and keep it in a place visible from where you work or where you will see it daily. Follow a person around for a day, you will learn what their priorities are. If someone followed you all day, what would they learn? How do you want to change how you spend your time?

Getting to the Good Stuff on the Playground Faster

My new job at Johnson Controls Automotive Group in 1992 was a wonderful opportunity to start up a centralized training department that would serve all staff functions at the headquarters and the 44 manufacturing sites in the United States. Here I was, I had never worked in a corporation before. I didn't know all the rules and conventions. I was used to running my own small business. I was energized and inspired to not only spread the best practices, but to enhance learning and improve performance of both employees and the business as a whole. As a business owner, I knew the importance of producing a return on investment. I saw so much that could be done. I felt like a kid on a playground. I wanted to run around, swing, climb the monkey bars, and try out the seesaw. My manager set some priorities and I felt like parts of the playground were restricted. I told her this. Her response was extremely helpful. She said, "I am helping you get to the good stuff faster." She was right. The priorities she set enabled me to focus on the important things. From my perspective, everything was shiny and new, and I wanted to go after it all. She showed me where to focus.

Story — Caroline

Introduction to Caroline

Caroline was a member of our women's visualization group in Albany, and is one of the most amazing women I know. She has transformed her life multiple times through the power of visualization and deep spiritual beliefs.

Caroline

Caroline, a beautiful and loving woman who greets everyone with a warm hug, was an administrator for the school district's special education program. Since childhood, Caroline had wanted to be an interior designer—she was enamored with everything to do with design and homes. She drew plans for beautiful spaces; she made huts, doll houses, and doll furniture; she was always focused on creating warm and livable places. In junior high, Caroline created a career to become an interior designer. She didn't know how to pursue that dream and her parents—wanting the best for her—encouraged her to go to a liberal arts school; she followed in the footsteps of her college football coach dad and majored in physical education at a rural college in New York State. Her dream of becoming an interior designer never left and Caroline dabbled in it periodically. In her 30's, still chasing the dream, Caroline took an interior design correspondence course and later took an adult education class in interior design. But, for the most part, life got in the way and other things took precedence, and over time her dream relocated to a remote corner of her mind.

Caroline married a man in the service; she followed him to an Air Force base in the Philippines. They returned to New York, and her husband went to Syracuse University for an MBA. Caroline felt that this might be her chance to pursue her dream! Syracuse University had a design school; she scheduled a meeting to discuss her application to the School of Interior Design. When asked to present her portfolio, she had nothing to show, and all her confidence in becoming an interior designer vanished! Immediately after leaving the office, she noticed the School of Education; she walked directly in and registered. She earned her degree in elementary and special education and later completed a Master's in Education Administration at SUNY Albany.

Caroline worked as a school administrator for many years and spoke passionately about the needs of the migrant families she served. She struggled with her dysfunctional manager who took the fun out of work. One of Caroline's friends wanted to do an experiment in visualization and goal setting and introduced her to a group of women creating their personal vision. Each month, ten to twelve women gathered to create a vision for their future using guided imagery, goal setting, and mutual support. Everyone was encouraged to write down their dreams and Caroline, then 47, found that her vision was extremely limited; when she tried to write, she became tied up in knots and struggled to list three things. The group continued to meet and practice visualizing. They would envision a magical journey into the unlimited future where anything was possible. At one session, participants met in groups of three and brainstormed magnifications of each other's dreams. The group excitedly explored and expressed limitless possibilities. The group enabled Caroline to see the possibilities. Caroline envisioned creating beauty through interior design. She could see herself designing spaces that brought peace and joy.

Reflecting on the process 20 years later, Caroline believes that these tools and God enable us to transcend our limited vision. "God sends us opportunities all the time and when the student is ready, the teacher appears. I use the same tools today and know there is higher guidance. It is not about success and failure; it is about trusting a deeper inner knowing and belief in a higher power that I am on the right path and all would be okay."

One exercise in particular was very powerful. In November, Caroline had been exploring plans for changing her career and even relocating. She thought she didn't have the background or the talent and did not know the way. She felt that she faced an insurmountable wall. Participants were asked to envision a beautiful garden and to follow a path. When guided to see a gate, Caroline saw a beautiful wrought iron gate that represented the obstacles she faced and feared. As she got closer to the gate, what had appeared a strongly fortified barrier became tissue paper, and she just walked through. She knew then that God would enable her to break through all obstacles.

She created a "Picture of Your Future" collage with a mirror in the center, pictures of different fabrics, houses, names of interior iesign schools, and locations to live. She set goals, identified the obstacles, and listed solutions to overcome them. She envisioned her life as an interior designer and all the benefits the new work and life would bring to her. She saw a bright, open, friendly world with numerous possibilities. That December, Caroline put her house on the market and in January resigned her job as a school administrator; she sold her house and moved in with a friend without knowing what was next. Later that month, a friend called and stated that she had found the perfect school for her, the New York School of Design. In February, the group discussed creativity and the process of creating one's own life. Caroline was realizing the benefits of overcoming long-term, self-limiting thoughts.

She moved to Manhattan in July 1990 and started two summer classes at New York School of Design. She thought she was an abject failure and cried the whole summer. Her first job was taking samples back for an interior design firm and she constantly felt intimidated by the design company. After working with an interior designer, Caroline worked for an architect and an antique shop. She started her own business in 1994 and designed the interiors of Manhattan condos and luxury beach houses. She purchased and renovated her own Manhattan condo.

Caroline was the first person I called during the terrorist attacks on 9/11. I was working in Cologne, Germany and was interrupted during a meeting at 3:15 pm with the news about the destruction of the Twin Towers. Driving home on the autobahn I called Caroline to see how she was. She answered the phone immediately and was shocked that anyone had gotten through. "How did you get through? No one has been able to get through!" Although not injured physically, that day marked a turning point and Caroline envisioned a calmer, more peaceful life upstate.

She rented a historic home in Hudson, New York, renovated it and created a highly successful bed and breakfast while selling real estate. Today, Caroline envisions a new career providing spiritual coaching and guidance.

Discussion

How did you feel about this story? What resonated with you? What did you learn about how this person created and implemented her vision? What could you apply?

Feelings	Thoughts that resonated with you

Action you will take

Creativity

As the chief creator in your own life, it is helpful to learn about creativity. The stages of creativity are defined as: preparation, incubation, illumination, evaluation, verification or revision, and completion.

Preparation: Preparation is a conscious process of collecting information, images, data, and possibilities. We file these away. Observe those experiences and people that make your heart sing. Brainstorm. Add these to your dream list.

Incubation: Incubation is the subconscious process that occurs during guided imagery, receptive visualization, meditation, sleep, and during flow. During these activities, we let go of our need to control a person, situation, or problem. The information we have filed away starts to percolate.

Illumination: Illumination frequently is experienced as an "aha." The solution or an inspiration spontaneously reveals itself. We get a sudden glimpse of the solution and have a feeling of certainty and joy. This moment occurs when doing something else like taking a shower, walking, enjoying nature, or some other physical activity.

Evaluation: Evaluation is a conscious activity that includes judging the pros and cons of each possibility and deciding which option is best to take.

Verification or Revision: During verification, we manifest the goal. This is a conscious process and includes writing the steps of the goal, implementing, and revising goals as opportunities and obstacles arise.

Completion: The task is finished at completion. This is a time to celebrate! Allow yourself to feel satisfied and fulfilled. Acknowledge and accept that you have realized your dream. Beware the feeling of sadness or depression for the loss of this dream now completed. After working hard and being "all in" on a specific goal, sometimes you might feel let down. Be sure to celebrate and then look towards your next challenge.

The Path of Least Resistance

In 1984, Robert Fritz published *The Path of Least Resistance: Principles for Creating What You Want to Create*.[46] Fritz draws on his experience as a composer to discuss the structure of the creative process. He provides three important insights to ensure progress: we take the path of least resistance as we move through life; the underlying structure determines the path of least resistance; and we can change the underlying structure of our lives. In other words, we have the power to utilize our circumstances to achieve our goals. Acceptance is empowering.

Think of the alcoholic who tries numerous ways of controlling their drinking but inevitably winds up drinking. When the alcoholic admits they are powerless over alcohol, they cease fighting it and the path of least resistance is to take the established steps toward a meaningful life of sobriety.

Once you have formed a vision of what you want, Fritz suggests you observe present reality relative to your vision. The disconnect between your desired vision and current reality causes tension and we seek resolution. Clearly define your current reality relative to the goal and magnify the discrepancy. Now, visualize your goal and in a split screen also see your current reality. You will move towards your highest dominant thought.

Fritz describes two structures: Oscillation and Advancing. Oscillation is a repeating pattern of advancing forward and then away from a goal, taking one step forward and several steps back. Think of the dieter who starves themselves and then binges. Advancing is a pattern of taking sustainable steps toward a goal until the destination is reached. You have a plan and must work the plan. To move towards our goals, we need to move from a reactive orientation to a creative orientation. Rather than reacting to circumstances, we envision what we truly want; we are responsible for being the creator in our lives.

What Does the Research Say?

We have already discussed a great deal of research that demonstrates how goal setting and guided imagery help to achieve goals and overcome obstacles. Specific goals produce specific results if we have the ability, are committed to the goal, receive performance feedback, and have the resources necessary to achieve the goal. To overcome obstacles and attain greater results, we must continue to focus on the goal, not let distractions get in the way, make an effort, be persistent, and have a strategy for success.[47]

To ensure positive change, we need to change our core belief system. Own your positive accomplishments to help build your inner belief and confidence. Each step you take towards a goal builds your belief that you can accomplish it. Visualizing a specific desired result aligned with your values gives you additional positive experiences that build your belief, increase your ability, and allow you to consider multiple strategies. In addition, guided imagery bypasses the prefrontal cortex and allows us to see the goal as the easiest path.

Neuroscience research establishes that not only do we follow the path of least resistance, but our senses trick us into believing it is the best choice. We see anything that takes more work as less appealing. We pick the apple that is the easiest to pick and then tell ourselves that it is the ripest and best apple.[48] When we continue to envision a task as already accomplished, it is the best choice.

> *"Creativity is intelligence having fun!"*
>
> — Albert Einstein

Action Steps

Directions: check each circle when completed:

1. Identify the resistance to accomplishing a goal and ask it why it is blocking you. ○
2. Go back to the goals you have set and identify obstacles and solutions. ○
3. Identify your top 5 daily priorities that will bring you closer to your goals. ○
4. Practice visualizing yourself having completed your goal while at the same time seeing where you are now. ○

Reflections

1. Write down all the ways in which you limit your desires and creativity. How are you not doing what you want? ○
2. Pray, let go, let God, and write. The answers will come. Put pen to paper and listen to the inner voice that comes from God. Practice spiritual writing and journal on the ways you limit yourself, obstacles, and solutions to your goals. ○

Module 8

Healing and Wellness

Objectives

At the end of this module, you will be able to:
- Identify opportunities for physical healing
- Describe how guided imagery can be used for healing and wellness
- Describe how visualization is used to reduce food cravings and to treat addictions
- Apply the steps of guided imagery to a specific pain
- Apply the steps of guided imagery to improve your health and wellness

Introduction

During this module, we apply what you have learned to health and wellness, a key part of sustaining an extraordinary life. You can let go of pain and sickness and move towards your ideal health. Research establishes the value of visualization and guided imagery in learning from your symptoms and your healing — and you will be able to apply this in your life. Let's move from embracing life to mastery of your well-being.

Celebration and Review

You have attained mastery in important areas of life and you live with gratitude. You have a vision for your future that you hold loosely with the full expectation that this or something better will be realized. You act from a deep sense of love and purpose and look for how you can share with others. Congratulations on letting go of the past and embracing yourself and your amazing life.

> *"There is a light in this world, a healing spirit more powerful than any darkness we may encounter. We sometimes lose sight of this force when there is suffering, too much pain. Then suddenly, the spirit will emerge through the lives of ordinary people who hear a call and answer in extraordinary ways."*
>
> *— Mother Teresa*

Have you ever felt a healing spirit? What does this quote mean to you?

Opportunities for Physical Healing and Wellness

Identify an area of physical pain that you would like healed. For example: headaches, knee pain, stomach pain.

Identify a wellness goal. For example: Lose 10 lbs., become more relaxed, decrease food cravings.

Guided Imagery and Disease

Jeanne Achterberg conducted studies on 126 patients diagnosed with stage IV metastatic cancer with life expectancies of less than 18 months. Various psychological tests and blood tests were administered and analyzed. After guided imagery and drawing exercises, patient attitudes were assessed regarding the cancer, its treatment, and any inherent ability to overcome it. The patients that drew pictures that showed healthy depictions of themselves predicted the change of the disease into total remission with 93% accuracy, while 100% of those that drew diseased depictions of themselves ended up experiencing rapid deterioration or dying by the two-month follow-up.[49]

Sixty-five women with breast cancer were given education on self-care, but only the experimental group of thirty-two women was trained in progressive muscle relaxation and guided imagery prior to chemotherapy. The experimental group listened to a recorded guided imagery for 7 days after chemotherapy. In just seven days, their symptoms of insomnia, depression, anxiety, and distress were significantly reduced when compared to the control group. [50]

Patients with cancer in palliative care benefited by guided imagery on multiple levels: physically (decreased pain, heart rate, and respiratory rate), spiritually (improved transpersonal relationships and freedom), and socially (improved interpersonal relationships). Confined patients reported missing nature and the freedom to move about, but by being transported to a field in the guided imagery they felt free and spiritually connected. [51]

Story — Lou

Introduction to Lou

I had the privilege to watch Lou as he grew in his career and family. After all, he married my sister. Lou has a positive mental attitude and is passionate in all his endeavors. Our family was shocked when Lou was diagnosed with cancer and I looked forward to his regular updates. Little did I know that he was using a special weapon to aid his fight. In addition to an excellent team of doctors and a strong belief in his health, Lou visualized a complete healing.

Lou

Lou had done everything right, and cancer attacked anyway. Lou knew success.

Lou, like many children of immigrants, was raised with a mantra, "Get an education, the more the better; no one can take away what is inside your head," his father always said. Lou's father also believed in the benefits of hard work, and Lou believes success is a decision. "If you don't get it, you didn't work hard enough."

Lou made his decision: he committed to being successful by making steady, measured forward progress. He worked hard and he benefitted. He excelled in school, he excelled in sports, he excelled in college, he excelled in business, and he married and had four boys. He was in good physical shape and stayed active as a triathlete, swimming, biking, and running regularly. He provided for his family in addition to caring about the community he lived in. He and his wife hosted numerous charity events to help those in need.

Lou, a corporate VP, learned leadership lessons from the sports teams he captained. His work ethic made him a standout, first on the field and later in business. Lou created a vision and shared it with his team, who followed it because they saw that he understood how to be successful.

In the summer of 2007, Lou had an earache and believed it was related to all his swimming. It kept hurting, so he sought medical treatment and was prescribed antibiotics and later steroids. When those failed, he was then referred to an ear, nose, and throat specialist. The ENT doctor said, "Lou, you have cancer." When the surgeon told him the tumor was too big to be safely operated on, Lou told everyone, "Good news! I don't need surgery." Meanwhile, the surgeon told Lou's wife that the tumor looked like an exploding cauliflower and was inoperable because it was too "bulky." The stoic surgeon pulled her close, telling her that with stage 4A cancer and that she and Lou should get their affairs in order. Lou worked with his doctor to design the most aggressive treatment possible.

A bowling buddy of Lou had survived cancer. The night before Lou started his treatment, the friend said, "I always saw in my head, my treatments were like a battle in Star Wars." During chemotherapy and radiation, Lou visualized light phasers shooting cancer cells that exploded. "It was like I finally had the weapons to fight back! Crazy right? I was just in my head, but it was literally my sole thought. I still keep it in my head in case I ever have to do this again, the weapons are better today."

Lou made everything positive. He never asked what stage cancer he had. Lou had stage 4 cancer of the esophagus. He did not look up survival rates and was unaware of the very poor chance of survival. He took the ominous, "it is inoperable," and spun it into a good story. He talked to an expert, a cancer survivor, and armed himself with phasers to fight cancer cells. Lou had a vision, Lou worked hard, and Lou defeated cancer. Today, he is living cancer-free with little to no side effects of treatment.

"Get an education, the more the better; no one can take away what is inside your head," Lou's father always said.

Module 8 — Healing and Wellness

Discussion

How did you feel about this story? What with you? What did you learn about how this person created and implemented his vision? What could you apply?

Feelings	Thoughts that resonated with you

Action you will take

Guided Imagery — The Healing Sun

Introduction to Guided Imagery

We will start with a guided imagery for relaxation and continue with a focus on each of the energy centers in the body.

The Healing Sun

Find yourself on a beach... feel the warmth of the sun... the light ocean breeze... Find a chair... a comfy chair just for you... Sit or lie down... Feel the warmth of the sun on your body. Allow the light and the warmth to penetrate every cell and organy.

Feel yourself relax into a quiet place inside yourself. This is a deep source of nourishment and healing for you. Ask, what do I need to do to heal myself now? What does my body need?

Know that you can heal.... You have limitless wisdom.... Say to yourself, "I am now healing. I am energized, alive, and filled with radiant health." Deep within you is a place that is all-knowing, all-loving, and all-wise. Allow this love and wisdom to flow throughout your body, your mind, your consciousness, throughout your very being... allow this love and wisdom to make your body feel good.

Guided Imagery — Opening Your Energy Centers

Introduction to Guided Imagery

In the following meditation, I will lead you through each of your chakras, or energy centers. You will envision the positive power of each area and will repeat an affirmation.

Opening Your Energy Centers

Lie down and allow yourself to relax. Take a deep breath and slowly let it out. Take another deep breath and slowly release it. The purpose of this guided imagery is to open your energy centers for deep relaxation and energy.

Imagine a ball of golden light on top of your head. Feel the spiritual energy and connection. Affirm, "I am an open vessel for love and light." Feel the light surrounding your head. Breathe deeply in and out several times, repeating the affirmation. I am a vessel for my higher power's love. I am connected to something much bigger than myself." See yourself radiating love.

Now, imagine a ball of light around your throat. Affirm, "My voice has power. My words have power, and I always choose to speak my truth. I speak up for myself with love and power." Feel the ball of golden light as you breathe in and out deeply. See yourself speaking up with power.

Imagine the ball of golden light over your heart, warming it, healing it, opening it. Affirm, "I love all of myself unconditionally. I deeply and truly love and honor myself. I give love. I receive love." Feel the ball of light as you breathe in and out several times, repeating your own version of an affirmation. See yourself with an open and loving heart.

Move your attention to your midsection, your solar plexus. Imagine a golden ball of light on your solar plexus. Affirm, "I am powerful and successful! I choose to take back my power from past situations and people. I allow my authentic self to shine." Feel the golden ball of light as you breathe in and out several times while seeing yourself as a powerful, loving person who accepts themselves exactly as they are.

See the ball of golden light over your belly, the sacral chakra. "Affirm, I let go of old wounds and am emotionally in balance. I accept myself and my life exactly as it is right now." Feel the golden light as you take several deep breaths. See yourself as emotionally centered.

Move your attention to the base of your spine, your root chakra. See an opening, clearing it, healing it, balancing it. Affirm, "I am supported by the world; all my wants and needs are provided for. I have a right to be here. I have a right to express and manifest my dreams." Feel the golden light as you take several deep breaths. See yourself grounded and easily manifesting your dreams.

Now, see the ball of light at your feet. Affirm to yourself, "I walk in love and serve others with the steps I take." See yourself being of service, bringing love and joy to others. Take several deep breaths.

See all the balls of light like a string of jewels all the way from your head to your feet, glowing and energizing you. Take a deep breath and imagine the energy moving from your head along the left side of your body to your feet, and then exhale as it moves up the right side of your body to your head. See this circulate three times. Now imagine the flow of energy from the top of your head down your front to your feet, and exhale from your feet up your back to your head. Circulate this energy three times.

Imagine the energy has gathered at your feet and feel it glowing and moving up the inside of your body to the top of your head, where it glows like the sun pulsating as a fountain of light, then moves down the outside of your body back to your feet. Repeat this several times.

Relax and see yourself as glowing energy, connected, loving, and powerful! You are connected, loving, and powerful!

Affirmations for Chakras

- **Crown**—"I am an open vessel for love and light. I am a vessel for my higher power's love. I am connected to something much bigger than myself."
- **Throat**—"My voice has power. My words have power and I always choose to speak my truth. I speak up for myself with love and power."
- **Heart**—"I love all of myself unconditionally. I deeply and truly love and honor myself. I give love. I receive love."
- **Solar plexus**—"I am powerful and successful! I choose to take back my power from past situations and people. I allow my authentic self to shine."
- **Sacral**—"Affirm, I let go of old wounds and am emotionally in balance. I accept myself and my life exactly as it is right now."
- **Root**—"I am supported by the world; all my wants and needs are provided for. I have a right to be here. I have a right to express and manifest my dreams."
- **Feet**—"I walk in love and serve others with the steps I take."

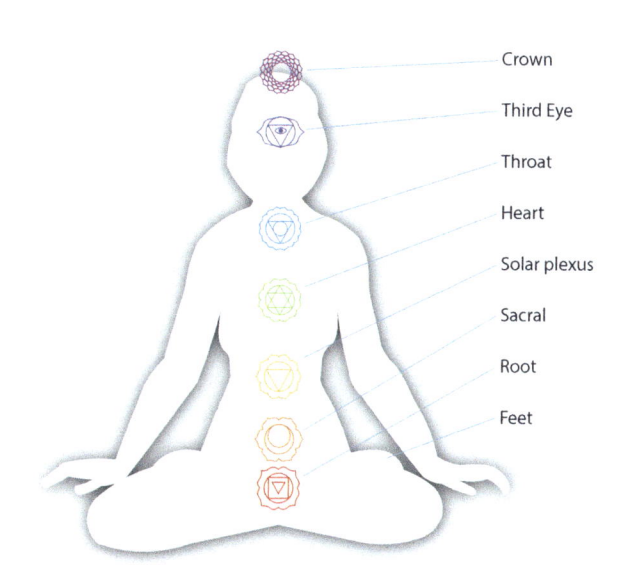

Crown
Third Eye
Throat
Heart
Solar plexus
Sacral
Root
Feet

Guided Imagery and Healing

Numerous research studies have demonstrated that guided imagery heals all types of conditions.

Carl and Stephanie Simonton theorized that by visualizing a robust immune system attacking the cancer, the immune system is stimulated. The Simontons and James Creighton published *Getting Well Again*[52]. They show how stress and emotional factors contribute to cancer and incorporate visualization and goal setting as methods to heal.

In 2002, Martin L. Rossman, MD, who would go on to co-found the Academy of Guided Imagery, became interested in imagery because it seemed to integrate the mind, body, and spirit. He uses a three-step method for dealing with patients: first, he tells them to go to a safe healing place, guides them with a healing imagery, then introduces them to their spiritual guides to access information they already have within.[53]

Five Steps to Healing the Body Through Guided Imagery

The following steps to healing through guided imagery provide a simple yet effective process for healing.[54]

1. **Relax.** Use a relaxation exercise.
2. **Imagine how the pain or illness looks and feels.** Is it hard or soft? Big or small? What color and shape is it?
3. **Be curious.** Ask the pain or illness questions about its purpose and what needs to happen for it to leave.
4. **Envision the pain or illness leaving your body.** Send love to the pain or illness and to the place where it was.
5. **Visualize healing.**
6. **Express gratitude** for the healing, knowing that it is in process.

Should I work with my doctor and take medications as prescribed while practicing guided imagery? Yes! Of course you should see a doctor. Guided imagery is a complementary medical intervention.

Guided Imagery — Listening to Your Symptoms

Introduction to Guided Imagery

This guided imagery will enable you to access knowledge about your symptoms and insight into how to reduce them.

Listening to Your Symptoms

After taking a comfortable position, relax deeply with a progressive relaxation script.

And, to relax more deeply, to become quiet in mind and body ... imagine yourself in your special, quiet place ... a special place of peacefulness ... serenity ... and beauty ... take a few moments to look around and notice what you see there... and what you hear in this special place of peacefulness ... serenity. Notice any odors or aroma. Notice a feeling of peacefulness ... find the spot in which you are most comfortable... and become centered and quiet ...

When you are ready, direct your attention to the physical symptom or problem that has been bothering you ... your symptom may be a pain, weakness, or dysfunction in some part of your body, or a mood or emotion that is uncomfortable for you ... as you focus on the sensations involved, allow an image to appear that represents the symptom ... simply allow the image to appear spontaneously, and welcome whatever image comes ... it may or may not make immediate sense to you ... just accept whatever comes for now ...

Take some time just to observe whatever image appears as carefully as you can... if you would like—bring the image into focus, make it more clear ... make the image brighter, more vivid ... notice details about the image. What is its shape? Color? Texture?... Density? ... How big is it?...How big is it in relation to you? Just observe it carefully without trying to change it in any way... How close or far away is it? ... What is it doing?

Watch the image ... notice any feelings that come up, and allow them to be there ... look deeper ... are there any other feelings present? When you are sure of your feelings, tell the image how you feel about it—speak directly and honestly to it (you may talk aloud or silently) ...

Then, in your imagination, give the image a voice, and allow it to answer you ... listen carefully to what it says ...

Ask the image what it wants from you, and listen to its answer... ask it why it wants that. Ask, "how would my life be different if I gave you what you want?" What does it really need? ... And let it respond ... Ask it also what it has to offer you if you should meet its needs ... Again, allow the image to respond ...

Observe the image carefully again, is there anything about it you hadn't noticed before? ... Does it look the same or is it different in any way? ...

Now, in your imagination, allow yourself to become the image... What is it like to be the image? ... Notice how you feel ... what thoughts do you have? ... What would your life be like if you were this image ... Just sense what it's like to be this image...

Through the eyes of the image, look back at yourself ... what do you see...Take a few minutes to really look at yourself from this new perspective ... as the image, how do you feel about this person you are looking at...what do you think of this person? ... What do you need from this person? Speaking as the image, ask yourself what you need ...

Now, slowly become yourself again...the image has just told you what it needs from you ... what, if anything, keeps you from meeting that need? ... What issues or concerns seem to get in the way? ... What might you do to change the situation and take a step toward meeting the image's needs? ...

Allow an image to appear for your Inner Advisor: a wise, kind figure who knows you well ... When you feel ready, ask your advisor about your symptoms and its needs, and any thoughts, feelings, or circumstances that may make it hard for you to meet those needs ... Ask your advisor any questions you might have, and listen carefully to your advisor's responses ... Feel free to ask your advisor for help if you need it ...

Now, mentally review the conversation you have had with your symptom and your advisor from the beginning ... If it feels right for you, choose one way that you can begin to meet your symptom's needs—some small but tangible way you can fill some part of its unmet needs ... If you can't think of any way at all, ask your advisor for a suggestion ...

When you have thought of a way to begin meeting its needs, recall again the image that represents your symptoms ... Ask it if it would be willing and able to give you tangible relief of symptoms if you take the steps you have thought of ... If so, let the exchange begin ... If not, ask it to tell you what you could do in exchange for perceptible relief ... Continue to dialogue until you have made a bargain or need to take a break from the negotiating ...

Consider the image once more... Is there anything you have learned from it or about it? ... Is there anything that you appreciate about it?... If there is, take the time to express your appreciation to it ... Express anything else that seems important...

Now, imagine your hands gently removing the pain ... Fill the space with healing light and love... Put the pain or symbol on a shelf; you can always pick it back up ... You need a rest from the pain ... Healing has begun ... You can now return to this room ... Slowly come back to your waking state and take some time to write about your experience...

Guided Imagery Reflections

Take a few moments to jot down any thoughts or feelings that occurred to you during this meditation. Did anything surprise you? How did you feel?

Story — Linda

Introduction to Linda

I have shared some of my story throughout this book and would now like to share more. For anyone suffering from addictions, I want you to know that you too can recover. I am grateful for my extraordinary life!

Linda

This is a story about God and God's grace. I feel so blessed.

I sat with Bill on the dock at my grandparents' lake home on a beautiful summer day. It was one of those days when anything seemed possible. I would be a consultant to businesses and help women to improve their lives; he would stay home with our beautiful, smart children. At 23, Bill is the Renaissance man. He makes everyone he meets feel comfortable and like themselves better. We would buy an old house and fix it up—notwithstanding that we didn't even own a hammer, much less know the difference between sheetrock and joint compound. We would travel the world, and all who entered our home would feel the love and joy. Bill had recently graduated with a degree in Asian Studies and Anthropology, and I would graduate with a bachelor's in Social Welfare. Bill was in the restaurant business, and I was doing direct care with developmentally disabled adults in community residences.

A year later, I listed my goals and dreams: maintain a wonderful relationship with Bill, run five miles daily, be a role model for women, be healthy and spiritual, run growth groups, be involved in community, go on bicycle trips, obtain grants, be articulate and a good public speaker, fix up a house. I added bake cookies and bread and make soups. Take a 2–3-week bicycle trip; be more thoughtful of others, more joyous, more sincere, and more prayerful; be more thankful. Some long-range goals included running long distance, teaching workshops, and writing books.

Two years later, Bill and I bicycled for 3 weeks around Nova Scotia, from Yarmouth to Halifax. It was the coldest June on record, and we put socks on our hands in the morning so that we could move our fingers. We had a wonderful adventure!

Bill had a mentor who inspired him to dream—his restaurant co-worker, Al, said, "Son, I am going to make you a millionaire." He taught Bill how to save his money and invest in housing. After our wedding, Bill bought a 4-family house built in 1900. We would live in the one-bedroom apartment and rent out the two 2-bedroom apartments and a 4-bedroom apartment. We immediately started renovating our apartment. Let me clarify: I started knocking down walls with some good friends, drunk out of our minds. When Bill returned from work at the restaurant, I was plastered in white and he could see the back wall. The next morning, hungover, I realized we didn't know how to fix it, we didn't even own a hammer. Other good friends helped Bill learn how to sheetrock, tape, and finish walls.

I took a class in Transactional Analysis and was especially intrigued by a participant who introduced himself as a business consultant. When I asked him to tell me more about what he did, he offered to meet with me and my manager. We were sold and immediately registered for a class in Time Management. The class motivated us, greatly improving our productivity. *Hmmm,* I thought. *I could teach this to the entire management team at Living Resources*; I called the number on the training materials and explained my interest. I received a return phone call and the pleasant man asked if I ever considered becoming a consultant. "YES! I want to become a consultant," I responded enthusiastically. He offered to send me a round-trip ticket to fly to their headquarters and would pay for two nights lodging, only if I would come and learn about the business. Bill told me not to buy training materials, so I came home having invested the down payment for our next house in a distributorship. I was 25, a social worker, had never worked in a business, and didn't know anyone who owned a business. I had 40 boxes of inventory in our now beautifully renovated tiny apartment. I hadn't counted on the selling that would be required and found it quite different from my previous sales experience selling Girl Scout cookies. I had a wonderful coach, Kenneth, who patiently asked each week, "How many phone calls do you plan to make? How many appointments will you have?" In a few months, I was fulltime in my own business, Training Dynamics. I was teaching others to write down their dreams and to set written and specific goals while I do the same. I am a product of the product!

As I was learning to sell, I was recruiting and training a sales force. I leased office space at the swanky major bank. At one point, I was overcome with feelings of defeat from receiving a long series of "no's." I practiced envisioning a red carpet with trumpets announcing my arrival. I imagined the prospective customer saying, "Where have you been? I have been waiting for you all of my life!" It was easy to imagine as I walked up that long sidewalk into the office of a manufacturer. The owner listened to the first ten minutes of my presentation and exclaimed, "Where have you been, I have been waiting all of my life for you!" He immediately enrolled two of his people in my course on Motivational Management!

In less than a year after starting my business full time, my deep feelings of inferiority peeked out from under my grandiosity. I had been drinking daily for ten years and felt like a fraud. I was teaching others to set and realize their goals and I was not making progress towards mine. In fact, I hated myself and just wanted to disappear. I thought, *maybe I should check to see whether I was an alcoholic*, so I opened my left-hand desk drawer and took out the business card from a place called AlCare. I had put it there months ago; I made the call. The counselor told me that I had probably been an alcoholic for some time and could start treatment after the 4th of July. In the meantime, I was told to go to Alcoholics Anonymous meetings. I cried every day as I started the journey to recovery. A recovering alcoholic suggested that I try this way of life for 90 days and if I didn't like it, they would gladly refund my misery. This, I understood. I did not know how to live without drinking. I cried every day. I still had a business. I was not making much money. I no longer drank. My last drink was July 20, 1984. I worked the program and was recovering one day at a time.

Over the next three years, I grew the business up to seven sales associates, had the swanky office, some sales, and I was thinking, "this goal setting really works." I really learned how to visualize. I then envisioned global work—consulting all over the world. In addition, Bill and I still imagined having children, but the time was never right. In May 1987, I hit a major barrier: seven salespeople quit in the same month. Totally demoralized, I could not do the work to build up the sales organization again. It had taken four years to get to that point. The lease just happened to be up at the end of the month. I could not continue. I closed the office. The men in the office next to mine bought my furniture, and I moved my stuff into the house. The business was over. I was finished. *What now?* I thought.

A hard rain was falling as I drove home from a meeting with my sponsor; my tears and anguish mirrored the storm. I turned it over to God. She said, "I have something special for you." A feeling of peace and love enveloped me. In the next three weeks, I received more business than I had in the previous five years. In three months, I was pregnant. A manager from General Electric (GE) found my company's name in the phone book and offered me what turned into three years of consulting work, most of it full-time. A "chance encounter" with the president of a think tank and conference center, turned into more than a year of exciting work on innovation in the public sector.

Then blessings of all blessings, my daughter Sarah was born. She continues to surprise and delight me with her intelligence and sophisticated sense of humor. I was leading "Train the Trainer" workshops for GE Plastics all over the country and received a contract from New York State to lead fourteen 4-day Train the Trainer workshops throughout the state for government employees.

With gratitude for all my blessings, I felt led to start a group for women in recovery to help them envision a better future. As we met monthly in the living room of my home, I felt encouraged and supported, my relationships with these women deepened, and my dream list grew. I had then listed my dream to visit every major city in Europe, Mexico, South America, and Asia. Other than Canada, I had never been outside the country. Getting a passport and figuring out how to get some place foreign and pay for it seemed overwhelming, but I envisioned myself feeling more and more comfortable. In my mind's eye, I could spin a globe and put my finger anywhere on it. Traveling to any location in the world would just be that easy.

My next pregnancy ended in miscarriage after 13 weeks, and I was devastated. I felt as though my heart had been ripped out. My business wasn't so important, and I decided to let go and let God; after applying for three jobs, I landed a job leading training for a global automotive supplier in Michigan. We moved to Ann Arbor. There I was, with a corporate job and managing two people! I was amazed. I felt like a kid on the playground: everything was shiny, inviting, and fun. I had been given the opportunity to start up a training department at a global corporation with 44 US locations. With my small team, we developed and implemented programs in leadership development, engineering, team building, and lean manufacturing. Bill stayed home with Sarah, and just as Sarah was getting ready to start school, I became pregnant with Anna, who was born that November! Another blessing! Anna has taught me about the importance of comfort and that it is okay to get cozy with a blanket and a good movie. I have learned much from her social intelligence, and I am inspired by her social conscience.

After six years, the Vice President of Human Resources offered me a position to lead learning in Europe: to start up and implement the same kinds of programs I had implemented in the US for 80 locations in 14 countries in Europe. In February 1999, my husband Bill, daughters Sarah and Anna (ages ten and four), and I, moved to Düsseldorf, Germany. We found a beautiful home: a renovated 300-year-old farm by the Rhine River in the town of Kaiserswerth, the site of a castle built in the 11th century. I was given a BMW as my company car. Each weekend, we visited a new city, country, art museum, castle, or church all over Europe. Of course, my work took me to many cities such as Barcelona, London, Paris, Prague, and Lisbon. On our own we travelled to Ireland, the Greek Island of Samos, spent a week skiing in the Austrian Alps, celebrated the new millennia in Rome, Florence, Pisa...

Now, forty years have passed, and when I awake each morning, I thank God for my life exactly as it is right now, ask that I be freed from self-seeking and self-pity, and that I be guided on how I can be of service to God and my fellows. I am blessed with a loving family; Bill, who has been a stay-at-home dad and later a teacher; Sarah, a partner in a law firm; and Anna, a social activist working for the The Humane Society of the United States. When we gather on a typical Saturday morning, you will find us in the kitchen baking bread or cookies. Perhaps a pot of soup is already simmering. We have travelled and have friends from all over the world. I have been sober for 36 years, run five miles a day, and am healthier and stronger than when I was in my twenties. I have overcome three job losses and many more shifts in employment. I have survived breast cancer and the loss of loved ones. I am grateful for the loving support of our friends and family. I am a business performance improvement consultant and work with women to create and realize a compelling vision for their future. God is truly good!

Discussion

How did you feel about this story? What resonated with you? What did you learn about how this person created and implemented her vision? What could you apply?

Feelings	Thoughts that resonated with you
Action you will take	

Module 8 — Healing and Wellness
Reducing Food Craving and Addictions

Have you ever had the experience of having a craving for food, drugs, or alcohol in which you vividly imagine the substance and every part of your body is screaming, "I want this!!"? Perhaps ice cream pops into your mind and you start noticing how the ice cream tastes—you want it! You start decorating that dish of ice cream with a banana, whipped cream, chocolate sauce, and sprinkles. The more you imagine the ice cream sundae, the more you crave it. You can't get it out of your mind. We call this Elaborated Intrusion Theory (EI Theory). Using this theory to understand what causes these cravings, we can reverse-engineer the process to overcome them! By practicing vivid visualization of healthy goals and the subsequent feelings of wellbeing, self-satisfaction, and positive responses from others, your desire for the healthy is increased while the craving is weakened.[55,56]

The following is another example: Audrey receives negative feedback from her manager and immediately feels stressed; her heart races and she finds difficulty breathing. An intrusive thought enters her mind: "a glass of red wine would be good for my heart and would relax me. It would be very helpful." She elaborates on this thought. She pictures the bottle and the glass. She sees herself pouring the wine into the glass and taking a sip, then that reassuring "click" that will tell her everything is okay. Audrey has been sober for over a year and values her sobriety. She pictures her sponsor and the other sober women she admires. She sees herself connecting to God and to the other women. She sees herself as a good mother and wife and elaborates on this image, feeling good about herself. She is a good worker and has a fantastic job, sober. The thought of the drink has been replaced. She calls her sponsor and talks about it.

What does the Research Say?

Research demonstrates that guided imagery has a positive effect on healing by reducing stress and anxiety, decreases pain, increases the quality of life, enhances immune response, improves sleep, improves psychological factors, enhances spirituality, increases the rate of healing, decreases the amount of pain medication taken, and decreases patient length of hospital stay and costs.

Cocaine addicts who practiced visualizing their lives without cravings for cocaine, reduced cravings and use of cocaine and other drugs.[57]

Guided imagery improved the psychology and quality-of-life for gynecologic and breast brachytherapy patients.[58]

Breast cancer patients undergoing chemotherapy listened to a guided imagery recording for 20 minutes each day for seven days and experienced decreased depression, insomnia, physical symptoms, and pain. [59] Another study showed that relaxation and guided imagery had a positive effect on women undergoing chemotherapy for advanced-stage breast cancer, showing an enhanced immune response.

In a study involving 134 patients undergoing cardiac surgery, guided imagery decreased the length of hospital stays by an average of 1.5 days, decreased stress and anxiety by 41.3%, decreased pain, improved sleep, reduced pharmacy costs (such as direct pain medication, saving $288.51 per patient), and reduced the cost of the procedure from an average of $11,743 in the control group to $9,761 in the experimental group. One week before surgery, patients were provided with two guided imagery recordings set to music designed to guide them to a relaxing, safe place and were encouraged to acknowledge any negative feelings. They listened to the recordings several times a day during the week prior to surgery and one to two weeks after surgery. On the day of surgery, patients listened to relaxing music from arrival to administration of anesthesia and then again after surgery. Guided imagery is now part of the hospital's clinical care process. [60]

During the COVID-19 pandemic of 2020, patients with COVID who used guided imagery showed reduced pain, anxiety, heart rate, systolic blood pressure, and oxygen saturation, showing that guided imagery is a cost-effective complementary therapy for COVID. It increases relaxation and boosts patients' immune systems to fight against COVID-19. [61]

Module 8 — Healing and Wellness

Action Steps

Directions: check each circle when completed:

1. Identify goals for personal healing. Where do you feel pain in your body? ○
2. Identify goals to improve your wellness. Would you like to become more fit or strong? Would you like to eat healthier foods? ○
3. Apply the steps of guided imagery to a specific pain. ○
4. Apply the steps of guided imagery to improve your health. ○

Reflections

1. Journal on how you would feel if in the highest state of health and well-being. ○
2. Journal on how healing could help you accomplish your goals. ○

Module 9

Enhancing Skills and Performance

Objectives

At the end of this module, you will be able to:

- Make time to do what is important to you
- Identify goals for enhancing performance and skills
- Identify reasons for not making the progress you want to be making
- Identify how guided imagery enhances performance and skills
- Assess yourself on wheel of life to identify additional areas of focus

Introduction

We will apply the tools of this program to all important areas of your life to achieve outcomes beyond your wildest expectations. You deserve an extraordinary life. A professional athlete applies the skills of visualization and continuously strives to up their inner game to achieve excellence. You surround yourself with excellence and apply all that you have learned to specific areas, whether it is a sport or physical activity, mastering emotions and moving towards ideal emotional health, creating deeper, meaningful connections with family, friends, and the community, growing spiritually, creating greater financial independence, or contributing your talents to soul satisfying work.

Celebration and Review

You are achieving amazing results in your life! Congratulations! You no longer react to life's ups and downs because you have the power to choose how you will respond. You accept your life exactly as it is right now. You live artfully and are filled with awe and wonder. No longer stuck in the past or fearing the future, you enter fully into this present moment. In the previous module, you set goals to improve your health and well-being. Dreams you envisioned have sprung to life!

Personal Mastery

Creativity requires vision and mastery. As the artist creating your own life, you need both. It takes hours of practice to develop mastery of any skill. The following quote from Peter Senge defines personal mastery

> *"The discipline of continuously clarifying and developing our personal vision, of focusing our energies, of developing patience, and of seeing reality objectively."*
>
> *— Peter Senge*

Mastering Your Life Design

Your life is perfectly designed to produce the results you achieve! If you are not happy with the results, it is time to change the design.

Your feelings influence your thoughts, your thoughts lead to how you will act, and your behaviors lead to the results you achieve. Let's start with the end in mind and the results you want to create in your life.

Feelings ➡ Thoughts ➡ Behaviors ➡ Results

My husband and I drove to the Great Smoky Mountains National Park to explore and photograph the scenic wonder and to enjoy the serenity and peace of nature. We decided to drive the 11-mile one-way loop around Cades Cove, nestled in the Smoky Mountains. Soon after we entered the one-way road, we realized we were going very slowly. Start, drive 4 miles an hour, stop for a couple of minutes, and so on, for 20 minutes on a near-empty tank of gas.

An hour passed... We were frustrated. I told myself we were going to run out of gas. I panicked. "This is not right," I exclaimed indignantly! "I am going to call the Park Headquarters." I picked up my phone. "Something is wrong and they should fix it!"

My husband tells me to put the phone down.

"I am going to give the park a poor review!" I exclaim, getting more amped up.

My husband shouts he is going to give the park 1 star. And every tree and mountain gets one star.

"Well, I am giving no stars," I said.

And then we were laughing. Each new declaration was more ridiculous! After 40 minutes, a park ranger walked by and apologized for the hold up; bears were in the middle of the road. We stopped at a historic cabin and had a picnic in a beautiful field! We enjoyed the peace and serenity of nature and just being with each other. We were in a bad situation; we were frustrated by forces beyond our control, but we decided to use what we had—each other—to turn it around into a positive and memorable experience.

You have a vision that includes the results you want to achieve, what you are doing, thinking and feeling. Design your own life, so that you will follow the path to **your** dreams, not someone else's.

For the past 30 years, I have worked with businesses to achieve outstanding results through the application of goal setting and human performance technology. I am a Certified Performance Technologist. I apply a systematic approach to improving human performance. It is an evidence-based integrated approach that draws from many disciplines including organizational behavior, change theory, psychology, instructional design, organizational design, and behavioral science. By applying this process to your life, you will achieve the results you desire. Let's apply it to an individual—YOU!

Analyzing Your Life Design

What are the results or outcomes in your life that you want but have not realized? Why are you not making progress? Do you have a process? Take a look at your current process, and determine where the disconnects are. We are going to look specifically at mastering time management by implementing a regular planning process. We will review the factors that make good goals and identify ways to increase your skills. Then we will look at the inner game, your habits of thought.

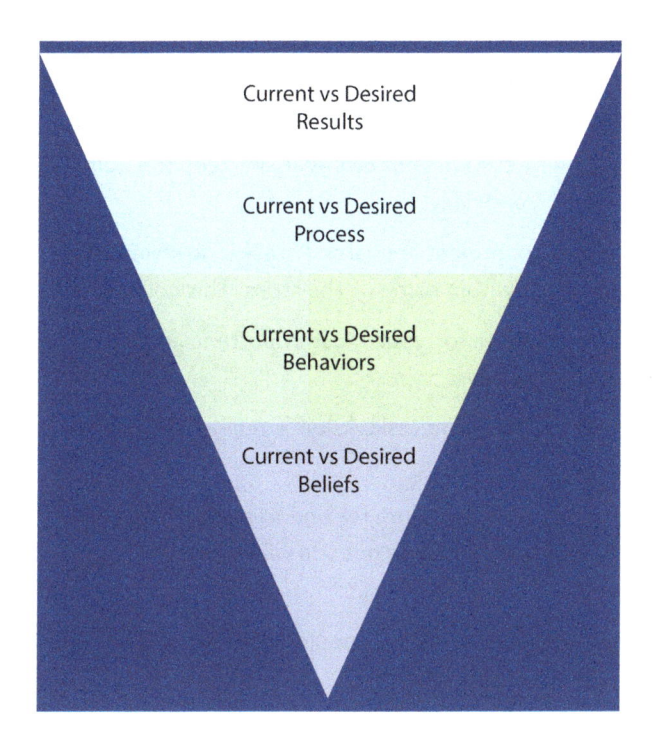

```
        Current vs Desired
             Results

        Current vs Desired
            Process

        Current vs Desired
           Behaviors

        Current vs Desired
             Beliefs
```

Start with the results you want to achieve; identify the reasons for gaps between the current and desired state. Identify any poorly defined processes and the behaviors needed to improve the process and achieve results. Identify the necessary beliefs to achieve the desired behavior. Beliefs determine whether we will succeed or not.

Your life is perfectly designed to create the results you realize. If you are not happy with the results, change how you design your life.

Analyzing Gaps in Results

Why aren't you getting the results you want? When working with organizations, the primary reason they are not getting the results they want is because they do not have a process to do so. Often, I begin to improve an organization's process by initiating time management training. While it was designed to achieve business results in an organization, we can apply the same methods to individuals for personal results!

Module 9 — Enhancing Skills and Performance

Mastering Time Management

In Module 5, we learned about a system of planning that included annual, quarterly, monthly, weekly, and daily planning. This is the best way to ensure you will make time for the most important things. Let's apply some actions:

1. Schedule planning time in your calendar and keep this commitment to yourself: monthly, weekly, and daily.
2. Identify each major project or goal and break it down into steps. You will probably have smaller steps within some of the steps. This could look like an outline.
3. Create a daily tracker for your most important goals. This helps create habits that lead to your success.
4. Prioritize each project and task. Ask if it really needs to be done and eliminate it if not.
5. Track how you spend your time for one week. Identify and eliminate (or reduce time on) any activity that does not add value to your life or the accomplishment of your goals.
6. Identify tasks that someone else could complete and delegate or hire someone else to do it.
7. Identify the tasks for the day and group similar tasks—phone calls, emails, errands, shopping.
8. Create a sense of urgency to accomplish the tasks by setting a time limit for its completion. We tend to take up the time available. You don't make all your time available.
9. Avoid procrastination by scheduling 10 minutes to start work on the task. You will probably continue working on it once you get started. Reward yourself.
10. Avoid other time wasters like constantly checking your social media, email, or phone. Use your desire to do one of these things as a reward for completing a difficult or unpleasant task.
11. Check off each task once completed. Get an endorphin rush.
12. Celebrate!

Mastering Emotions

You know who you are and what values are important to you. You take full responsibility for your own actions and strive for excellence. You have let go of the past and more fully show up in the present moment.

Feelings come and go; things happen that we don't like and can't control. We cannot control other people, what they say, think, or do. We can only control our reactions to them. We cannot control gravity or the weather. In the Serenity Prayer, we ask for the serenity to accept the things we cannot change, the courage to change the things we can, and the wisdom to know the difference. I repeat this prayer throughout the day. Acceptance is the answer. When I accept my life at this moment exactly as it is, I experience peace and serenity.

The story we tell ourselves can make the difference between empowering and emboldening ourselves or letting fear, doubt and worry take over. Mindfully, watch your feelings without judgement, let them come and go. Notice when you get especially disturbed by what you are telling yourself about the situation. You can change the story. You are in charge of the narrative you tell yourself. "Move a muscle, change a thought," even if it is cleaning or walking the dog. What are some ways you have learned to change from negative emotions to positive?

I use the following to help me:

Gratitude—Meister Eckhart, a 14th century mystic, says that if you utter one prayer, 'thank you' would be enough. Think about all the good that has entered your life and make a decision to be grateful. This provides an immediate happiness boost.

Oneness and Wholeness—Remember that we are all connected! We are connected to Mother Earth and one another. In creation-centered spirituality, we see the Holy Spirit in everyone and everything. We open our hearts to connections, to all peoples everywhere.

Forgiveness—Resentment is a powerful emotion that prevents us from connecting to God and to inner peace. Let go and forgive yourself and others. At this moment, we are all doing the best we can.

Curiosity—Develop a sense of curiosity about the possibilities in your life. Curiosity inspires and motivates us to move beyond our current state, to learn and grow. When negative emotions dog your every step, curiosity is the best way out. It moves us beyond thinking about ourselves and our pitiful circumstances.

Visualizing Your Best Possible Self—Many of the guided imageries are designed to have you imagine your best possible self. Both counting one's blessings and seeing one's best possible self help to increase happiness.[62]

The Power of Vision—Remember the vision you have for the future and know that it is already being made manifest. Read stories of others who have accomplished the unbelievable. See how the power of vision impacted Oprah Winfrey in the below story.

Oprah Winfrey

In the 1980's, Oprah reads the novel, *The Color Purple*, and becomes obsessed with it. She tells everyone to read it and suspects there will be a movie someday. She pictures herself in the movie. At that point, she was a local radio and television news host with no prior acting experience. One day, she gets a casting call to read for a movie called "*Moonsong*." She auditions and is asked to read for one of the main parts. She plays opposite a character named Harpo, which is Oprah spelled backwards. She takes this as a sign that she will get the part.

When she doesn't hear anything, she calls to see if a decision is made and is told by the casting agency that they make the calls, not her. "We have real actresses reading for the part." She thinks they don't want her because she is fat. She is ashamed. She goes to a fat farm. She is running on a track and decides to let it all go. She surrenders by singing Judson W. Van DeVenter's song, "I Surrender All." Right then, she gets a phone call. It's Steven Spielberg, who is calling to personally offer her the part. Not only that, but she learns that *Moonsong* was, in fact, a production codename for *The Color Purple* adaptation all along. When she thought she was only working her way up to her dream role, fate would have it that her dream would be fulfilled when she needed it most.

Guided Imagery — The Labyrinth

Introduction to Guided Imagery

A labyrinth is an ancient symbol that relates to wholeness. It combines the imagery of the circle and the spiral into a meandering but purposeful path. The Labyrinth represents a journey to our own center and back again out into the world. Labyrinths have long been used as meditation and prayer tools.

The Labyrinth

Take a slow, deep breath, expanding your chest and abdomen. Pause a moment, then exhale slowly, feeling your chest and abdomen relax. Breathe in this way until you begin to feel quite relaxed. As you become more relaxed, your breathing will become slow and even. You now feel calm and comfortable.

Feel your feet and legs. Imagine them becoming very heavy. Say to yourself, "my feet are relaxing, they are becoming more and more relaxed... My feet are deeply relaxed." Feel your ankles, lower legs, and thighs. Imagine them becoming very heavy. Say to yourself, "my ankles, lower legs and thighs are becoming more and more relaxed. They are deeply relaxed." In the same way, relax your stomach, chest, back... Say to yourself, "I am becoming more and more relaxed..." Relax your hands, forearms, upper arms, and shoulders. Feel them becoming very heavy. Relax the muscles of your neck and jaw, allowing your jaw to drop. Relax your face, your tongue, eyes, and forehead. Enjoy the feeling of total body relaxation. You are now in a calm, relaxed state of being.

You are about to begin a journey ... A journey into the labyrinth ... This journey will have many spirals and twists and take you on your path... these steps are a metaphor for your inward journey ... and will take you where you must go ...

Feel the warm sun and let it heal you ... Let God's love embrace you ... I invite you to experience the uniqueness of your path. You are on your spiritual journey, to connect to the sacred, to find meaning and direction ... See the dirt path ... it is a large circle ... as it takes a large curve outward ... the path is marked by low hedges. As you walk the outer path, meditate on the you that others see ... See how you want others to see you ... Allow yourself to feel good about your accomplishments, your strengths ... the circle is coming back into a close.

As you come to the first inward turn to the next circle, pause to express gratitude for all that you have and are. Let go of the need to please others... of any expectations you have for yourself... You are enough, you have enough, you do enough! You have everything you need. Let go of any resentments or negative feelings ... Let the gentle breeze carry them away ... If a specific resentment comes up, forgive the person ...

Continue on the next circle and concentrate on the beauty around you. Stay in the moment. Look at all things with awe and gratitude ... You are part of this whole ... Open your heart ... feel the love ... embrace the divine in all things...

You come to the next inner circle. Pause. Is there anything you need to release? Release it and let the gentle breeze carry it away ... Is there anyone you need to forgive? Forgive now ...

Continue on the next inner circle. Meditate on your inner self, who you think you are ...

You come to the last inner spiral, release anything you don't need.

Arrive at the sacred center. See a mirror. In this mirror, you will see how God sees you ... a perfect child of God, loving ... You discover or affirm an inner truth, a purpose ... Now it is time to go back out into the world and carry that truth and awareness to the world ...

Take the path back out of the Labyrinth. See how you can use what you learned ... your purpose ... you may see a symbol or hear a whisper.

Meditate on this as the path carries you outward ... See what God wants for you. God's ideal ...

You are now outside the Labyrinth... See the steps that will return you to the here and now... with each step you will feel more and more alert ... step 1, 2, 3, feeling more and more alert ... step 4, 5, 6, hear the sound of my voice and notice your breathing ... 7, 8, 9, feel the chair ...10 ... you are now back in your room. Wiggle your toes and your fingers. Gently and gradually open your eyes...

Guided Imagery Reflections

Take a few moments to jot down any thoughts or feelings that occurred to you during this meditation. Did anything surprise you? How did you feel?

Analyzing Performance

Are you making the progress you want to be making? On the goal sheet, you listed obstacles and then identified solutions. Let's look more closely at common reasons we don't do what we are supposed to do. The diagram is called a fishbone diagram and is a common problem-solving tool. On each of the branches (or "bones"), write down the reasons for the gap in performance related to this topic.

1. Lack of clear expectations.
2. Lack of consequences or incentives.
3. Lack of information and feedback.
4. Lack of environmental support and resources.
5. Lack of individual capacity.
6. Lack of motivation.
7. Lack of skills or knowledge.

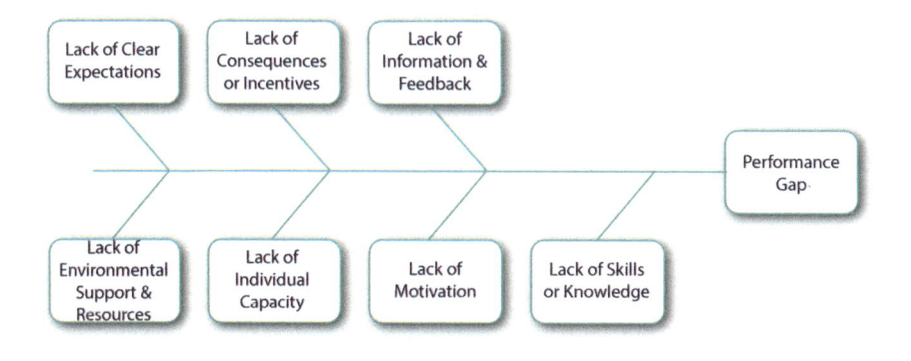

Clear expectations.
You know exactly what, when, and how much needs to be done. The number one reason we don't do what we are supposed to do is because no one told us to do it. Perhaps your goal is too hazy. Remember: clear, specific goals produce specific results.

Consequences or incentives.
What incentive or reward will you get when you accomplish a daily, weekly, or monthly task? Build in something that motivates you to take action. This daily discipline will create a habit, and soon you won't even need to think about it.

Information and feedback.
You know whether you are on track or not. You have a system for tracking your progress each and every day. The endorphin rush you get from accomplishing the task motivates you. Checking off the daily accomplishment builds confidence and belief.

Environmental support and resources.
Make sure your environment is conducive to accomplishing the tasks. Surround yourself with an environment and people who support you. Put your vision board and your goals where you can see them.

Individual capacity.
This is a reality check. I am 65 and I am never going to run an under-6-minute mile. Admit it, you might not have the capacity to reach your goal.

Motivation.
Make sure the reason you are working on a goal is powerful. Build your desire by listing the benefits for achieving the goal, make sure it is difficult (slightly beyond your grasp), yet attainable, and creates a sense of urgency. Just do it, and do it now!

Skills or knowledge.
Talk to others with the skills or expertise you want. Watch people with the skills and strive to imagine yourself performing the same actions. Visualize yourself with those skills. Continuously read, learn, and develop your skills.

Module 9 — Enhancing Skills and Performance

Identify any beliefs that contribute to causes for not doing what you want to or should do. How can you up your inner game?

For each reason, you are not doing what you would like to be doing, identify a solution.

Causes of Gaps	Beliefs

Solutions

Wheel of Life

Let's revisit the areas of your life that we explored in Module 2. Reassess where you are now in each area of life, relative to where you want to be. Imagine that the center of the below diagram represents 0 and the end of each spoke represents 100% achievement of your dreams in this area. Place a point along the continuum to represent where you stand now in that area. Connect the points. Is your life in balance? What areas need attention?

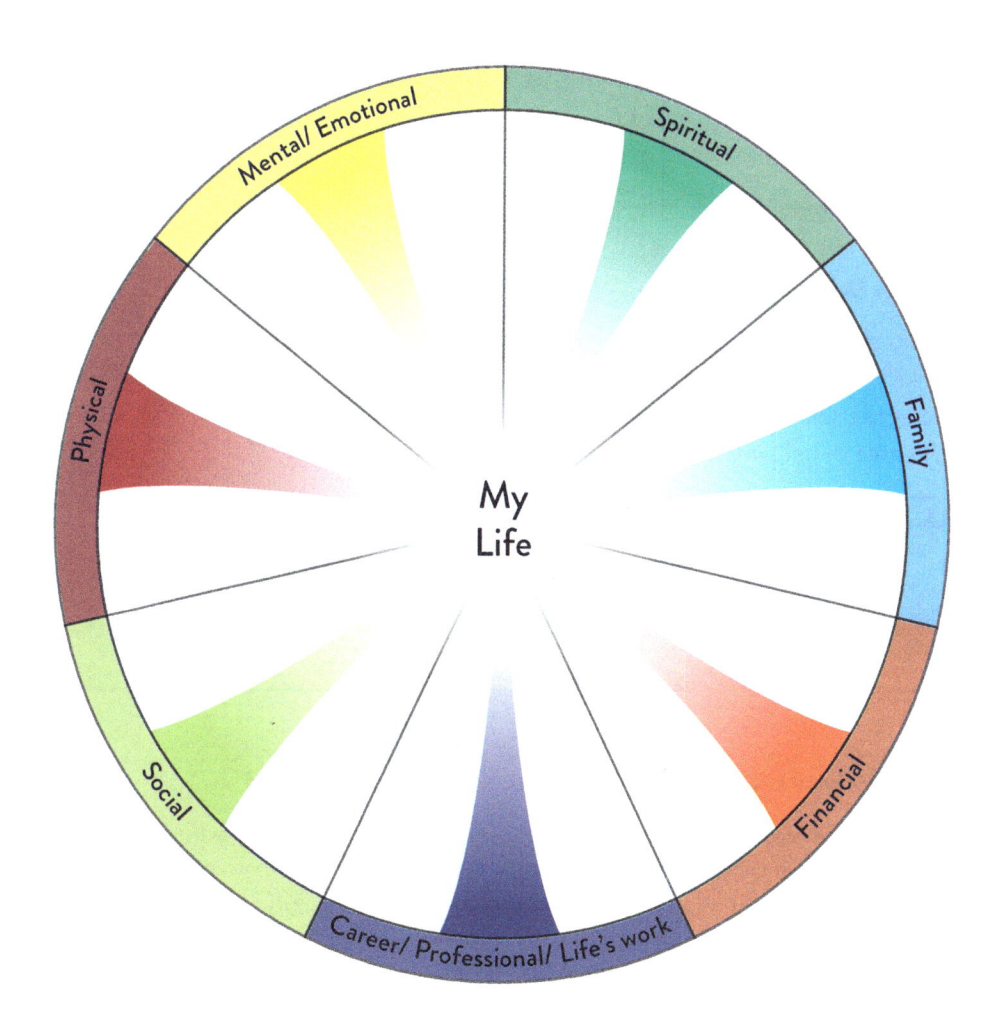

Mental/ Emotional
Spiritual
Family
Financial
Career/ Professional/ Life's work
Social
Physical

My Life

Goals for Improvement

Identify an area where you would like to achieve better results and improve your performance. By performance, we mean our behavior plus the results or outcomes of that behavior.

Examples include improving time management, finishing a book that you have worked on for 10 years, investing money, starting or leading a business, or committing to a fitness or healthy eating regimen.

Goal to Achieve in 90-Days	Desired Result	Skills Needed to Improve
Example—Improve time management skills	Eliminate 4 hours a week of non-value-added time and use for something more value added	How to eliminate waste. How to plan daily.

Goals for Skill Improvement

Identify a skill that you would like to perform better. Determine the best way to learn this skill. Don't forget to use the people on your team for help. Find someone who is good at the skill you want to learn. Go inward and ask your inner helper with mastery in this area to help improve your skill.

Identify the steps to learning the skill.
1.
2.
3.

Mental Practice and Performance

The same brain areas involved in the unconscious planning and performance of a task are involved when we envision performing the task.[63] Mental practice or visualization has been well-established as a method to improve performance in a number of different fields: sports, dance, and exercise, and is a characteristic of successful people. It has been demonstrated to improve strength. When mental practice was combined with physical practice, performance improved even more. Mental imagery practice should be used to supplement physical training or used to replace physical training when practice is not possible.[64]

Story — Deb

Introduction to Deb

I have known Deb all of her life; she is my sister. Deb has demonstrated the power of manifesting through visualization, positive beliefs, and faith. Through high school, sports meant watching our brothers play soccer or baseball; since college, Deb has developed strength, speed, perseverance, and grit by competing in numerous Ironmans, triathlons, and marathons. She truly enjoys empowering athletes by providing the tools for proper nutrition for optimal health and athletic performance.

Deb

My sister, Deb, is 8 years younger than me. I have a vivid memory of 2-year-old Deb standing on the stone stoop of the neighbor's back door. She had wandered over, just wanting to say hi. It is a sunny, mid-August day and very hot. She stands at the door, waiting and waiting. No answer. She screams, still standing by the door. The neighbor opens the door, picks her up, and brings her home. My mom puts her on the couch and takes care of her. Soon, each of her tiny feet are covered with huge blisters. My heart goes out to her. In the same room, my 12-year-old sister Lori is celebrating her birthday with several friends as a slumber party. Deb lays on the couch like a princess.

When I was in my early twenties and Deb was 15, I remember visiting my family and noticing that Deb spent most of her time in her room. She may have eaten with us or taken a plate up to her room; she was restricting herself to 550 calories a day. She had an eating disorder and was very thin. She was not physically fit. Yet, in November of 2020, Deb completed her 9th Ironman in Cozumel, Mexico: a strenuous competition that begins with a 2.4-mile swim, followed by a 112-mile bike race then a complete marathon of 26.2 miles.

How did Deb go from living in her bedroom, barely eating, to successfully completing 9 Ironman competitions, 12 half Ironmans, 100 sprint triathlons, over 25 marathons and over 40 half marathons?

In high school, Debbie started running to get some exercise, and later attended State University of New York at Plattsburgh where she earned a BS in Nutrition Science. She envisioned herself healthy, fit, and strong, helping others with eating disorders. While in graduate school at Syracuse University studying Exercise Science, Debbie met some bicyclists and started joining them on rides. They were joined by a woman who excitedly shared her success in completing an Ironman in Kona, Hawaii. When the woman had gotten to the registration desk to pick up her packet, she was questioned about whether this was something she was able to do. They didn't believe that she could complete it. At that moment, Deb sees herself at the registration table at the Kona Ironman. No one questions her ability. They all know she can do it. She sets a goal to complete a marathon; this is a tall order at that time. In her 20's, Deb finishes her first marathon after her son Austin is born. Every two years for the next six years, she has another son. Now with four sons, she starts a chapter of a nonprofit exercise group for mothers, and soon she inspires hundreds of moms who join for weekly runs and motivation.

Deb starts swimming in her 40's and completes her first Ironman in 2008. In 2010 and 2011, injuries prevented her from training. Since then, she completes one Ironman a year, plus marathons and half marathons.

Deb visualizes every aspect of the competition, from start to finish. She imagines feeling calm, strong, and light. She imagines herself passing people to get ahead. In the Ironman, she envisions the transitions: completing the swim, putting on her helmet, and getting on the bike, then docking it away for the final run. She imagines the timer at the finish line flashing her goal time. She absolutely knows she will finish!

Deb inspires all who meet her, from young moms running for the first time, to adolescents with eating disorders, diabetics in a community health setting, to experienced endurance and competitive athletes. She has worked hard, accomplished much, and truly enjoys giving back by empowering athletes with the proper nutrition for optimal health and athletic performance. I am grateful she is my sister.

Discussion

How did you feel about this story? What resonated with you? What did you learn about how this person created and implemented his vision? What could you apply?

Feelings	Thoughts that resonated with you

Actions you will take

Olympians Using Visualization

Search Google for Olympic athletes who use visualization and more than 700,000 results will pop up. Elite athletes use imagery to hear the audience, feel the wind, imagine past successes, and program success for future events. They feel every turn on the bobsled, every move by an opponent, every dive, every part of the gymnastic routine. They hear the roar of the audience. They imagine every step to receiving the medal and the weight of it around their necks.

Michael Phelps spent two hours in the pool daily, visualizing the pool, the water, the audience, and every stroke. He visualized potential obstacles and saw himself overcoming those obstacles.[65] Phelps has earned 28 Olympic medals, including 23 gold medals, more medals than anyone in Olympic history. Phelps visualizes a race hundreds of times before it begins so that when it comes time to start, his body knows exactly what to do.[66]

Story — Colonel George Robert Hall

In the 1960's, Robert Hall attended the University of Mississippi for one year and was then appointed to the Naval Academy in Annapolis, Maryland, where he participated in collegiate golf competitions and eventually became captain of the golf team. Like many young men, he was deployed to Vietnam, where he was shot down over the northern territory, captured, and put in the Hanoi Hilton prisoner of war camp. There, he was physically and mentally tortured, as well as starved on 300 calories a day. His physical world consisted of a 7 ½-foot cell where he was imprisoned for over seven years.

Six weeks after being released, he was asked to play in the 1973 Greater New Orleans P.O.W. ProAm Open and shot a 76. When asked how he could have scored so low when he hadn't played golf in the years he spent captured, he replied that he had played every single day in his mind over the past seven years. He envisioned his home course, saw each hole, calculated the wind speed, gripped the golf club, set up his swing, struck the ball, heard the sound, and saw a perfect shot.

Guided Imagery — Mental Rehearsal of Skill

Introduction to Guided Imagery

Mental imagery increases motivation, helps us to learn skills, and primes our actions to get us ready. Mental rehearsal uses your emotions, and the kinesthetic feeling of moving your body, as well as the sights, smells, and sounds of the environment. In this guided imagery, you will work on one skill or performance goal. The more you practice through mental rehearsal, the greater the benefit!

Mental Rehearsal for Skill

Think of a time when you felt especially confident and masterful. Choose one skill or performance goal. Envision a master performing this skill. See what this person is doing, and how this person is moving ... Watch carefully ... Listen to what that person is telling themselves ... Now, become the master. Feel how good it is to be competent in this skill ... Experience the emotions ... See yourself repeating the skill ... Notice other people and their response to you ... They are amazed! Do what a person with this skill does. Feel the strength and power of your skill. Every time you practice, you are increasing your skill and eliminating fear, doubt, and worry. Make the image more colorful, hear the sounds you might hear, and smell the sweet fragrance of success.

Guided Imagery Reflections

Take a few moments to jot down any thoughts or feelings that occurred to you during this meditation. Did anything surprise you? How did you feel?

What does the Research Say?

Mental practice has been well-documented to enhance skill performance, learning of motor skills, motivation, and self-confidence. Thirty-seven studies on mental practice were published between 1995 and 2018. They concluded that mental practice continues to have a positive impact on performance.[67] When imagery is combined with physical practice, performance is better than physical practice alone. Imagery practice enhances learning and performance as well as motivation.[68] Imagery effects are dosage specific; the more you mentally practice, the better the results.[69]

Jesmy Jose and Maria Martin Joseph reviewed nineteen research studies done during 2000–2017 to determine the effect imagery had on psychological variables and performance.[70] The studies indicated that imagery improved sports performance in volleyball, archery, basketball, golf, badminton, rugby, high jump, football, long-distance running, and much more. Most of the studies included a minimum of six weeks of imagery-based training or more. Training for less than a week didn't show much improvement in performance, but three days was enough time to show improvement in psychological variables such as anxiety, self-confidence, imagery ability, self-efficacy, and attention.

Action Steps

Directions: check each circle when completed:

1. Master time management, starting with planning daily. Do this for 21 days. ○
2. Identify opportunities for skill improvement and incorporate a regular practice of mental rehearsal to improve. ○
3. Identify reasons for not making the progress you want to be making. ○
4. Take steps to address the reasons for gaps. ○

Reflections

1. Journal on the ideal performance for your selected area. Describe it under ideal conditions. Describe what could go wrong and how you would handle under those conditions. ○
2. Journal on how you feel about your accomplishments. ○

Module 10

Boldly Follow Your Dreams

Objectives

At the end of this module, you will be able to:

- Describe the dreams and goals you have accomplished
- Identify the most important dreams you want to manifest
- Envision yourself as the hero in your own journey
- Review and update your vision for the future
- Implement specific goals

> *"Let the beauty of what you love be what you do."*
>
> — Rumi

Introduction

We will look again at creating or updating our vision for the future. You will identify more dreams and set and implement specific, challenging goals. You will experience a guided imagery to discover your passions and another to experience you as the hero in your own journey.

Celebration and Review

Congratulations! We have come full circle. You have created an extraordinary life. You have experienced a breakthrough toward success and have stepped into a new way of being; you are living a purposeful and meaningful life that only you can fulfill! You possess strong personal power, self-confidence, and self-esteem. You set and realize new goals and visualize your extraordinary future while living deeply centered in the moment.

Guided Imagery — Discovering Your Passions

Introduction to Guided Imagery

Let's explore and appreciate all of the experiences that make your heart sing and give you joy. You will experience a world of abundance and beauty.

Discovering Your Passions

Relax.

In this experience, you are encouraged to play and discover your passions. Those things that make your heart sing, that let you know that God is with you—the still small voice that brings you joy, love, laughter. This is a world of abundance. There is enough for all of us. Your higher power is the unfailing, unlimited source of your supply. As Meister Eckert says, "God is thousands of times more ready to give than we are to receive." These gifts are available for you to use, share, pass on, and then receive more.

Let us play with some images, with all of our senses. Remember a time when you were struck by the beauty of nature ... bring the image into focus ... Take some time to imagine all the beautiful details, and see yourself fully enjoying and appreciating it. Now, begin to walk (or fly, if you like) and see yourself in a totally different environment ... Your favorite place in the world ... What did you do there?

When you were in your teens—what music did you listen to? ... hear it now ... how did you feel?... dance to the music...your whole body is alive with joy...

Imagine going into a bookstore... Go to the section of the bookstore that attracts you... are these the books you enjoyed as a teen?

Remember a time when you felt healthiest... strong... relaxed... comfortable... Participating in a sport or exercise you enjoy...

Remember your favorite meal ... Imagine eating it again ... smelling ... tasting ... savoring it ... you baking or cooking...

A time when your heart sang with joy...

Art ... you creating art ... touching the materials, the medium ... The creation ... the feelings of creatively expressing yourself ... viewing art ... a time you were struck by the work of another artist ...

History ... an old church ... a castle ... a cobblestone street ... a museum...

See the face of a baby and that wonderful baby smell ... the face of a loved one ... The warmth of time with a friend ... a time when you gave of yourself ... your time ... your talents ... a special cause ...

A mental challenge and an aha... Learning... Subjects you are most interested in learning more about ...

People you admire ... Places you would like to go ...

Now, consider the areas we have reviewed and identify an area you are most passionate about ... whatever comes to mind—a picture or thought is right for you ... Follow that passion and see where it leads ... See yourself fully engaged and enjoying it ...

Enjoy it thoroughly. There are infinite possibilities. Eventually come home happy, content with the realization that the universe is truly a place of incredible wonder and abundance, and that you are ready to accept all the joy and prosperity life has to offer.

Guided Imagery Reflections

Take a few moments to jot down any thoughts or feelings that occurred to you during this meditation. Did anything surprise you? How did you feel?

> *"The most successful leader of all is the one who sees another picture not yet actualized."*
>
> *— Mary Parker Follet (1868-1933), American Social Worker and Management Theorist*

How do you Prepare to Live a Fuller Life?

Slow down, pray, envision your own life, family, community, and planet as a whole. Write down those dreams. To discover higher purpose, focus on those filled with light and love. Listen for that still small voice, the nudge of the universe and the Holy Spirit. Pay attention to what gives you joy, to the synchronicities. Live in the Kingdom, in the present.

Ask your Higher Power to guide you. Put pen to paper and write down dreams for living a fuller, richer, and happier life. Write in a stream of consciousness without judging or lifting your pen off the paper.

Module 10 — Boldly Follow Your Dreams

> *"The mind, once stretched by a new idea, never returns to its original dimensions."*
>
> *— Ralph Waldo Emerson*

Identify your Inner Advisory Board

Imagine that you have a group of inner guides you can appoint to your inner advisory board. Consider your dreams and goals; think about the assistance you could use. Let your imagination expand. Your inner guides may include: Cheerleader, Healer, Midwife, Finance Expert, Coach, Spiritual Guru, Visionary, Leader, Relationship Expert, Mystic, Creative Genius, Caregiver, Stylist, Intellectual Stimulator, Joy Maker. Your guides can also be actual people, dead or alive, who you admire and believe you can learn from. List the inner guides who could provide you with support and expertise.

My Inner Advisory Board

List the tasks for a major goal and identify the people who could help you with support and expertise.

Major Goal—Tasks	My External Advisory Board

High Points of My Life

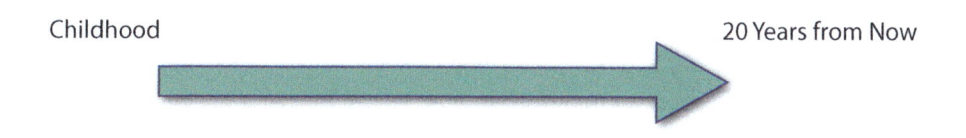

Childhood → 20 Years from Now

Low Points of My Life

Timeline of Your Life's Peaks and Valleys

Draw a line in the middle of a piece of paper. Identify the high points of your life on the top half of the paper and your low points on the bottom half of the paper relative to how high or low. Or if you prefer, record any turning points. Write a word or a phrase to describe the event and the date it occurred. Imagine the accomplishment of your greatest dreams and place them on the timeline too.

Guided Imagery — The Hero's Journey

Introduction to Guided Imagery

The purpose of this guided imagery is to enable you to experience your life's ups and downs as a mythical journey where you are the hero.

The Hero's Journey

Take a deep breath. And another deep breath. Allow your abdomen to rise and fall. As your breathing becomes slow and even, you will feel more and more relaxed. Now, relax your whole body in stages by whatever works for you. You will feel mentally alert and stay mentally alert. You are in control. Your body will feel warm and heavy. Deepen this feeling of relaxation by slowly counting backwards from 10 to 1. 10, 9, 8, 7, 6, 5, 4, 3, 2, 1.

Module 10 — Boldly Follow Your Dreams

Go to your special, sacred space and let yourself totally relax. I will give you a few moments to create that space. View your surroundings and make any adjustments needed to make yourself feel more comfortable and peaceful. This is where you can experience all that is good, loving, and wise. You are here to connect to God and to become your highest self for the good in the world. Matter, time, and space are unlimited... You have everything you need!

You are the powerful hero in the middle of your journey. You have experienced both highs and lows, deep sorrow, difficult challenges, and struggles. Let's focus on one of these, pick whatever comes to mind ... See yourself and experience what it was like to be in the valley of darkness ... See a bridge... this is your bridge ... It can be short or long ... any color you choose ... Cross the bridge ... You receive a call to follow a new way ... Hope glistens ... You let go of destructive or unhelpful habits and beliefs... You experience the love of your higher power ... Supporters join you on your quest and show you a better way of life one day at a time... Notice who these supporters are ... You experience unity ... You follow a way of compassion, mercy, joy, and love. You have been transformed and seek to bring what you have learned into the world ... See how you have brought this experience back into the world ... This is the Hero's Journey. There is more for you to do.

Hear the call of the Beloved, your Higher Power, or God! Accept this call and step into the continuation of the Hero's Journey.

Imagine a glorious being of light approaching you. Then, see this light standing directly in front of you! You greet each other warmly. This being represents your highest potentiality. Raise both your hands in front of you so that the palms are facing this being of light. Your palms touch. The being of light beams radiant love, compassion, wisdom, kindness, and strength and pours them into you. Receive. Step into your greatness... Thank the being of light. Listen, the being whispers to your soul and calls you on another adventure to fulfill a dream or purpose. All you have done up until now has prepared you. Imagine the adventure: the mountain you must climb... see what the mountain represents... see a waterfall ... stand under it and let all your limitations get washed away ... allies gather around you ... they encourage and support you ... you feel resourceful and powerful ... you are triumphant; you bring forth something new ... you take your place with all the strength, power, joy, love, and wisdom that is you ... Take some time to let this journey unfold in your mind's eye. Ask the being of light any questions you may have ...

Listen... Experience the emotions, the triumphs, the love, compassion, and joy. Know that you can return to this place anytime you wish. It is now time to return to this room and record what happened in your journal.

> "The universe is holding its breath waiting for you to take your place, no matter how humble that may be or how small that place may be."
>
> — Jean Houston

Mental Rehearsal of Goal Accomplished

Think of a time when you felt especially good. Choose one goal. See a movie of yourself in possession of the goal. Make the movie even more vivid — experience the emotions you feel, see yourself, and make the colors more vivid, the emotions sharper. Notice other people and their response to you in possession of your color. Notice the sounds, smell the fragrance of success. Touch... Mentally rehearse what you are doing to accomplish the goal. What are you doing because you have achieved the goal? See the consequences. Feel the power in you.

> "The journey of a thousand miles begins with a single step."
>
> — Lao Tzu

Story — Dennis W. Archer

Introduction to Dennis Archer

I introduced Dennis Archer earlier in this book and described how he created a mission in his life. He is a visionary leader who manifested a vision for his life and for the city of Detroit and beyond. He is an extraordinary man who engaged others in creating and implementing a vision for Detroit that turned Detroit around. Dennis Archer served as Mayor of Detroit from 1994–2001.

Module 10 — Boldly Follow Your Dreams

Dennis Archer

My company was hosting a large supplier diversity conference in Milwaukee and some of us, who had taken the corporate plane from Detroit, were talking in the hotel lounge. I was talking with the VP of Human Resources from my company and the President of the Michigan Minority Business Development Council where I had just started an assignment. A distinguished looking gentleman joined us. He embraced a couple of people and shook hands, calling them and more by name. He seemed to know everyone, and I was impressed with the personal qualities he demonstrated. Within four minutes it became very clear to me: here was a man with enormous influence and power who was passionate about justice and the rule of law. And, here was a man with tremendous love and respect for others.

Later, I learned that he had been born in Cassopolis, a town of 1,500 people in southwest Michigan, in a home with a dirt floor and no indoor plumbing. Each month, the family made the 15-mile trip to the barber's, and it is here that this man heard words that would be forever indelibly etched in his mind. The barber looked at the boy of eight years and said, "You are special. You are going to help a lot of people." The words and voice of the barber would pop into his head many times and influenced him to seek opportunities where he could be of service—to teach, practice law, serve on the Michigan Supreme Court, lead the city of Detroit as mayor for two terms, find time throughout to mentor numerous young people, and then to establish a scholarship fund. He continues to be guided by that vision of providing service to others. This man, Dennis Archer, has had an incredible impact on many people. Archer told me that he wasn't sure if it was actually the voice of the barber or the voice of "the big guy upstairs." He doesn't consider himself a religious person. Yet, he has honored many faiths and throughout his life has attended various churches: AME, Baptist, Presbyterian, and Roman Catholic. When he had a difficult decision to make—he would often look for wisdom in the Bible.

Although born and raised in poverty, Dennis Archer credits his parents for instilling in him the value of education. As a boy, he dreamed of being a teacher; he earned a Bachelor of Science degree in Education from Western Michigan University, then he taught learning-disabled children at two Detroit public schools from 1965–70. After teaching for a couple of years, he dreamed of having more impact on the children in his school and decided to become a principal. He attended the University of Michigan to obtain a master's degree and qualify for that role. One day, he confronted his professor and persuasively argued that the graduate class should be more challenging; he had already read two of the books in undergraduate school. The professor, Trudy DunCombe, told him that he should be a lawyer and suggested that he should be in law school, not education. He explained that he didn't know what a lawyer did. He didn't even know any lawyers. In fact, he had never talked to a lawyer. She suggested a couple of lawyers he could talk to, and later he not only went to law school—studying evenings at the Detroit College of Law and graduating in 1970—he also married the woman who suggested it. She took her own advice and became a lawyer as well. Archer was named among the "100 Most Powerful Attorneys in the United States" by the National Law Journal in April 1985.

When he first applied for a job after law school at the Detroit law firm of Dickinson Wright, he was told that they didn't hire from Western Michigan University. However, Dennis would not allow this obstacle to impede on his success, and he worked hard until the next opportunity would arise. In 1985, Governor James Blanchard appointed Archer as an Associate Justice of the Michigan Supreme Court, and in the following year, Archer was elected to an eight-year term. In 1990, halfway through his term, Archer was named the most respected judge in Michigan by Michigan Lawyers Weekly. According to Archer, this was a comfortable role and one that he could have kept. However, Dennis Archer is a man of vision who believes in greatness for himself and Detroit, and who inspires greatness in those around him. He left the bench for more ambitious endeavors.

In 1991, Dennis Archer, with the assistance of the University of Michigan School of Urban Planning, wrote a paper entitled "Thoughts for a Greater Detroit."[71] He described a vision for a very different Detroit and circulated it to a thousand thought leaders and decision makers in the city. Thoughts for a Greater Detroit included education, transportation, health care, business, and reduced crime. Archer painted such a clear and compelling vision of what Detroit could become that it led to his being asked to run for Mayor, his election, and, ultimately, to Detroit's improvement. Richard C. Van Dusen, a former partner of Dickinson Wright, was the one to ask Archer to run for Mayor of Detroit, and, according to Archer, he ran on faith. During the mayoral campaign in October 1993, Dennis Archer wrote "A Vision and Strategy for City Wide Revitalization," [72] in which he stated "My vision for 2001, the goal I want to pursue is our city shining, bright, and vibrant." This report incorporated many of the same themes as "Thoughts for a Greater Detroit" and provided a more specific strategy. "My vision is based on a rational plan with a predictable outcome. In the past, there have been projects executed here and there that have not leveraged additional investment. The past projects had a single focus without being part of a comprehensive strategy—and some had failed. No, our vision and plan will make sense. We are going to invest in projects that expand our tax base through the creation of businesses, jobs, and livable communities. We will work together to design it with our eyes in the stars, but our feet firmly planted on the ground. We will pay attention to the basics." He was subsequently elected to two terms from 1994–2001.

The report, "Detroit: Building on a Solid Foundation A Community Vision for 2002-2010 dated April 11, 2001," [73] describes the progress Detroit made towards achieving the ideas and suggestions described in "Thoughts for a Greater Detroit," November

Module 10 — Boldly Follow Your Dreams

1991.

Some of the major impacts include: serious crime in the city of Detroit fell 22% from 1993 to 2000, homicides decreased 32%, preventive health care programs were developed and expanded, bus service was substantially improved enabling people to get to jobs, and unemployment fell from 13% to 6.8%. In December of 1994, Detroit was designated as an Empowerment Zone worth $100 million in U.S. aid over the course of 10 years, which would attract an initial $6 billion in new development, create more than 10,000 new jobs, and develop 1,500 new residential units. Contracts were awarded to minority-owned businesses, providing new opportunities for business owners and their mostly minority employees.

In 2000, Detroit won the bid to host the 2006 NFL Super Bowl XL; however Ford Field hadn't been built and the city lacked enough hotel rooms. During the Archer administration, major development projects revitalized downtown Detroit and included the Compuware world headquarters, Comerica Park, Ford Field, three casinos, rebuilding the theater district, and renovating the General Motors World Headquarters at the Renaissance Center, bringing new jobs and new tax revenues with them.

Dennis Archer was named among the "100 Most Influential Black Americans" by Ebony magazine, one of the "25 Most Dynamic Mayors in America" by Newsweek magazine, and "Public Official of the Year" by Governing magazine in 2000. Archer contends that numerous people helped him become who he is, and he strongly believes in giving back by being an active mentor to 75-80 young people over the years. While mayor of Detroit, he dreamed of giving back in a financial way as well. The Dennis W. Archer Foundation Scholarship awards scholarships to Detroit high school graduates to attend Western Michigan University or Wayne State. He hopes this foundation could be used "to make the difference for a significant number of Detroit high school graduates each year for as long as it is possible to imagine."

Dennis Archer is special and has helped a lot of people. He sought the opportunities to be of service to others. When the opportunities presented themselves, he seized the assignment, and when there was more than what one person could do, he painted a clear and compelling vision of the future to engage others. It wasn't one big event or challenge that made Dennis Archer successful, but the shining, bright, and vibrant promise of being special by serving others. May you seize the same promise for yourself! You are special and will help a lot of people!

The Fall and Rise of Detroit,
KatePepinArts.com

Discussion

How did you feel about this story? What resonated with you? What did you learn about how this person created and implemented his vision? What could you apply?

Feelings	Thoughts that resonated with you

Action you will take

> *"When nothing is sure, everything is possible."*
>
> — *Margaret Drabble*

Guided Imagery — The Door of Possibilities

Introduction to Guided Imagery

Welcome to the final guided imagery. Remember, you can go online and listen to the guided meditations in this book and more. In the following guided imagery, you will explore possibilities for your future.

The Door of Possibilities

Take a deep breath and allow yourself to relax. Take another deep breath and allow yourself to relax. Another breath, and you become more and more relaxed. Allow

Module 10 — Boldly Follow Your Dreams

yourself to be as you are. There is no right or wrong way to be. Today, we are going on a sacred journey. Take a deep breath, breathing in joy and light. Release any remaining negative emotions. Center yourself in the power, love, and wisdom of God. Sink down deeply to your center, your soul. Know that you are a whole spiritual being filled with love and light. Trust the process.

You are outside in the sunlight, following a path. Feel the sun at the top of your head and allow it to warm you. Notice a gently rolling hill with wide steps along the path. There are 10 steps and you are on the top, the tenth. With each step, you will become more and more relaxed. 9, 8, you go deeper and more relaxed, and your arms are feeling very heavy. 7, 6, allow your neck and face to relax, on the next step—5, your back and abdomen become more relaxed, 3, your legs feel heavy and deeply relaxed, 2, 1, you are alert yet relaxed, and you are open to possibilities …

You continue along the path and notice a waterfall. It is a hot day, so you walk behind it, feeling the refreshing spray. The water washes over you, washing away all limitations, rinsing away all doubt, anger, fear of lack. All negativity simply dissolves … Release anything else you no longer need … You feel renewed and experience a new sense of possibility, wonder, abundance, love, and forgiveness.

Continue along the path feeling the golden sunshine drying you, warming you, healing you. The path bends and you continue to follow. See a door. This is the door of possibilities, possibilities for your future. Open the door and walk in. Your heart opens and love shines all around you. The deepest longing of your heart has been fulfilled. It is now five years in the future, and you see how many of your dreams have been realized. You have been renewed and have an extraordinary life filled with joy. You embrace your wholeness and see abundance everywhere. See your relationships with your loved ones and some of the connections you have made…

You are loveable and see the highest in everyone you meet. See your friends and some of the things you have enjoyed together.

See one goal you feel especially good about completing … See the abundance in your life's work … Experience the positive emotions of fulfillment, gratitude, and so on … Notice the things you have been able to do or buy due to your financial success …

Your health and fitness have been much improved … You move fluidly, lightly, gracefully, wearing life like a loose garment … See yourself and feel how it feels to be fit and strong …

Spiritually, you have grown … Notice what that looks and feels like…

Emotionally, you have grown … Experience how that feels …

Mentally, you have learned much…Take stock of those things you have learned …

You have developed more healthy habits … See yourself go about your ideal day … I will pause and let you envision your day from the time you wake up ... Your morning ... Your afternoon ... Your evening .... Imagine your day in vivid color and strong positive emotions. Envision yourself happy, joyous, and free ... Take some moments to thoroughly enjoy this day.

Take a moment to review all the positive things from this mediation and know that it has already happened. Express gratitude for all you are welcoming into your life. Allow any thoughts, feelings, or pictures to emerge ... Whatever you experience is right for you.

Know that you can return to this space anytime. When you are ready, it is time to return to the room. Let's follow the path back to the stairs. Imagine climbing up the steps to the here and now. 1, 2, 3, become more alert, 4, 5, 6, hear my voice, feel the chair ... 7, 8, 9 ... wiggle your fingers and toes, 10, gently and gradually open your eyes.

Guided Imagery Reflections

Take a few moments to jot down any thoughts or feelings that occurred to you during this meditation. Did anything surprise you? How did you feel?

My Vision for My Extraordinary Life

Module 10 — Boldly Follow Your Dreams

Action Steps

Directions: check each circle when completed:

1. List the dreams and goals you have accomplished. ○
2. List the people on your inner and outer advisory board. ○
3. Identify the most important dreams you want to manifest ○
4. Describe yourself as the hero in your own journey. ○
5. What specific goals will you implement over the next 90 days? ○
6. Update your vision for the future ○

Reflections

1. Write down dreams for living a fuller, richer, and happier life. ○
2. Describe yourself as the hero in your own journey. ○
3. How does it feel to be the hero in your own journey? ○
4. What have been your greatest achievements during this program? ○

Conclusion

Congratulations! You have completed an amazing journey! Celebrate!

My hope is that you have stepped fully into your unique and extraordinary life! You deserve it. You have broken through self-limiting beliefs and obstacles to accomplish your most important goals and live happy, joyous, and free. You have listened to your heart to become the person you envisioned.

My journey began as a social worker and corporate learning leader where I developed a systematic approach to improving learning and performance. Over thirty years ago, I began leading monthly workshops for women using guided imagery and goal setting. Our hearts opened, we discovered dreams long buried, we set goals, we shared our feelings, and we held each other accountable. We were all amazed at the transformation in our lives; I had to write this stuff down! I researched goal-setting and guided imagery and designed a spiritual and systematic process built on the evidence. I drew from my experience leading learning in Fortune 100 companies, where I improved the performance of individuals, teams, and companies, helping employees find meaning in soul-satisfying work and helping companies save millions of dollars. The process works!

My firm conviction is that we all have the power to create an amazing life. I wrote this book for anyone who dreams of something better and wants a path to move to the next stage in life. My book guides you step-by-step with a process, tools, and action plans to create your unique, extraordinary life; it inspires you with stories of those who have succeeded, and enables you to tap into the wisdom and creativity of your subconscious.

We explored your vision and dreams for the future. We built a strong foundation with clear values, a defined mission and priorities. We charted our course by defining steps to reach long term goals and narrowed the focus until we knew what we needed to do today to reach our dreams. We broke free of self-limiting beliefs and habits that no longer served us and embraced new blessings and beliefs. We grew in mastery and applied the process to all areas of our lives. We broke through barriers that held us back and stepped into our new powerful way of being, taking our unique place in this world and living an extraordinary life!

Dear reader, I hope you continue this journey. Revisit each phase of the journey as you build mastery. Life is not linear nor are these phases. As you learn, grow, and enter new life stages, circle back to an earlier phase and apply learning in a deeper, more meaningful way. Here is a review of the transformation journey you have been following.

The Transformation Journey

Exploring
Call forth your creativity and direct the inner critic to step aside. Explore your vision and dreams for the future. Surround yourself with people and things that inspire you. See all the possibilities and you will have an abundant supply of dreams. Imagine that you will succeed.

Building a Foundation
Build a strong foundation to support your dreams and vision to create a life that truly matters. This requires deep insight that comes with opening your heart and soul and listening to your intuition. With a clear sense of purpose and set of values, you will be able to establish priorities for the life you want. Your commitment will grow!

Charting a Course
Focus on specific, worthwhile goals that are aligned with your vision, mission, and values. You will learn and apply proven strategies that propel you to action and accomplishment. You see yourself already in possession of your goals. You realize increased self-esteem, confidence, and clarity.

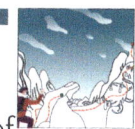

Embracing the Journey
Break free of inner constraints. Let go of self-defeating habits and emotions that no longer serve you and make room to embrace all the good that is entering your life. You will grow in self-belief and will rely more on your intuition. Even the obstacles and difficult terrain will provide opportunities for growth. Experience deep emotional and spiritual healing. Unencumbered, you readily discover new dreams and a new ideal for your future self. You embrace the journey, yourself, and even life itself.

Mastering Your Life
Envision and move toward the ideal you! Commit to excellence! You are the artist creating your own life. Apply the same tools and process to other areas of your life: mental, physical, social, family, financial, professional, and spiritual. You have achieved extraordinary results in your life and have embraced empowering beliefs. You feel increased vitality, joy, and serenity. You are mastering life and living your greatness!

Breaking Through to Success
The world has been holding its breath waiting for what only you can provide. You have broken through to success and have stepped into a new way of being; you are living a purposeful and meaningful life that only you can fulfill! You possess strong personal power, self-confidence, and self-esteem. You have created an extraordinary life. You set and realize new goals and visualize your extraordinary future while living deeply centered in the

Conclusion

moment.

The rating scale goes from a 1 meaning strongly disagree to a 5, strongly agree.

1	2	3	4	5
Strongly Disagree	Slightly Disagree	Slightly agree	Agree	Strongly Agree

1.	I have an abundant supply of dreams — ideas for what my future can become.	1	2	3	4	5
2.	I have written and specific goals.	1	2	3	4	5
3.	I know what my mission/ purpose is in life.	1	2	3	4	5
4.	I have a identified my most important values and principles for living.	1	2	3	4	5
5.	My priority goals are based on my mission and values.	1	2	3	4	5
6.	I know what kind of legacy I want to leave behind.	1	2	3	4	5
7.	I find it easy to visualize the dreams I want to create in my life.	1	2	3	4	5
8.	I can vividly see myself already in possession of my goals.	1	2	3	4	5
9.	I have a strong desire to create the goals I want.	1	2	3	4	5
10.	I practice visualizing the goals I want in life.	1	2	3	4	5
11.	I regularly say affirmations that support the goals I want in life.	1	2	3	4	5
12.	I always follow my intuition.	1	2	3	4	5
13.	I have clearly identified the benefits to achieving my goals.	1	2	3	4	5
14.	I believe that I deserve the goals I want to achieve.	1	2	3	4	5
15.	I have a vision board to support my goals.	1	2	3	4	5
16.	I have assessed where I am currently relative to the goals I want to achieve.	1	2	3	4	5
17.	I can clearly envision the ideal me.	1	2	3	4	5
18.	I can clearly envision the extraordinary life I want to create for the next 5 years.	1	2	3	4	5
19.	I have identified the obstacles to achieving my goals and identified solutions to those obstacles.	1	2	3	4	5
20.	I have an action plan for my most important goals.	1	2	3	4	5
	Total					

End Notes

Notes to Module 1
1. Ostrander, S., Schroeder, L., & Ostrander, N. (1994). *Superlearning 2000*. Dell.
2. https://womensgolfjournal.com/ask-annika/sorenstam-clubs-mental-game-swedish-food/
3. Wilson, W. (2001). Bill's Story. *Alcoholic anonymous* (4th edition). Alcoholics Anonymous World Services (pp. 8–14).
4. Lipton, M. (2003). *Guiding growth: How vision keeps companies on course*. Harvard Business Review Press.
5. Lipton, M. (1996). Demystifying the Development of an Organizational Vision. *Sloan Management Review*, , 37(4), 82–92. https://sloanreview.mit.edu/article/demystifying-the-development-of-an-organizational-vision/.
6. Masuda, A. D., Kane, T. D., Shoptaugh, C. F., & Minor, K. A. (2010). The role of a vivid and challenging personal vision in goal hierarchies. *The Journal of Psychology*, 144(3), 221–242. https://doi.org/10.1080/00223980903472235
7. Kim, J., Kang, P., & Choi, I. (2014). Pleasure now, meaning later: Temporal dynamics between pleasure and meaning, *Journal of Experimental Social Psychology*, 55, 262–270. https://doi.org/10.1016/j.jesp.2014.07.018

Notes to Module 2
8. https://www.youtube.com/watch?v=RxPZh4AnWy
9. Skovholt, T. M., Morgan, J. I., & Negron-Cunningham, H. (1989). Mental imagery in career counseling and life planning: A review of research and intervention methods. *Journal of Counseling and Development*, 67(5), 287–292. https://doi.org/10.1002/j.1556-6676.1989.tb02604.x
10. Marshall, R. C., & Farrell, I. C. (2019). Career guided imagery: A narrative approach for emerging adults. *Journal of Creativity in Mental Health*, 14(2), 193–204. https://doi.org/10.1080/15401383.2019.1586612

Notes to Module 3
11. Logel, C., & Cohen, G. L. (2012). The role of the self in physical health: Testing the effect of a values-affirmation intervention on weight loss. *Psychological Science*, 23(1), 53–55. https://doi.org/10.1177/0956797611421936
12. Cascio, C. N., O'Donnell, M. B., Tinney, F. J., Jr., Lieberman, M. D., Taylor,

S. E., Strecher, V. J., & Falk, E. B. (2015). Self-affirmation activates brain systems associated with self-related processing and reward and is reinforced by future orientation. *Social Cognitive and Affective Neuroscience*, 11(4), 621–629. https://doi.org/10.1093/scan/nsv136

13. Steele, C. M. (1988). The psychology of self-affirmation: Sustaining the integrity of the self. *Advances in Experimental Social Psychology*, 21, 261–302. https://doi.org/10.1016/S0065-2601(08)60229-4

Notes to Module 4

14. Locke, E. A. (1968). Toward a theory of task motivation and incentives. *Organizational Behavior and Performances*, 3(2), 157–189. https://doi.org/10.1016/0030-5073(68)90004-4
15. Locke, E. A., & Latham, G. P. (2002). Building a practically useful theory of goal setting and task motivation: A 35-year odyssey. *American Psychologist*, 57(9), 705–717. https://doi.org/10.1037/0003-066X.57.9.705
16. Ivancevich, J,M., and McMahon, J.T. (1982).The effects of goal-setting, external feedback, and self-generated feedback on outcome variables: A field experiment. *Academy of Management Journal*, 25(2), 359–372. https://doi.org/10.5465/255997
17. Becker, L. J. (1978). Joint effects on feedback and goal setting on performance: A field study of residential energy conservation. *Journal of Applied Psychology*, 63(4), 428–433. https://doi.org/10.1037/0021-9010.63.4.428
18. Bandura, A. (1982). Self-efficacy mechanism in human agency. *American Psychologist*, 37(2), 122–147. https://doi.org/10.1037/0003-066X.37.2.122
19. Locke, E. A., Frederick, E., Lee, C., & Bobko, P. (1984). Effect of self-efficacy, goals, and task strategies on task performance. *Journal of Applied Psychology*, 69(2), 241–251. https://doi.org/10.1037/0021-9010.69.2.241
20. Anderson, C.R. (1977). Locus of Control, Coping behaviors and performance in a stress setting: A longitudinal study. *Journal of Applied Psychology*, 62(4), 446–451. https://doi.org/10.1037/0021-9010.62.4.446
21. Locke, E. A. (1982). Relation of goal level to performance with a short work period and multiple goal levels. *Journal of Applied Psychology*, 67(4), 512–514. https://doi.org/10.1037/0021-9010.67.4.512
22. Locke, E. A., & Latham, G. P. (2019). The development of goal setting theory: A half century retrospective. *Motivation Science*, 5(2), 93–105. https://doi.org/10.1037/mot0000127
23. Judge, T. A., & Bono, J. E. (2001). Relationship of core self-evaluations traits—self-esteem, generalized self-efficacy, locus of control, and emotional stability—with job satisfaction and job performance: A meta-analysis. *Journal of Applied Psychology*, 86(1), 80–92. https://doi.org/10.1037/0021-9010.86.1.80
24. Latham, G. P. (2019). Unanswered questions and new directions for future research on priming goals in the subconscious. *Academy of Management Discoveries*, 5(2), 111–113. https://doi.org/10.5465/amd.2018.0195

25. Locke, E. A., & Latham, G. P. (2019). The development of goal setting theory: A half century retrospective. *Motivation Science*, 5(2), 93–105. https://doi.org/10.1037/mot0000127

Notes to Module 5

26. Agor, W. H. (1989) *Intuition in organizations: Leading and managing productively*. Sage Publications, Inc. (pp. 11).
27. https://womensgolfjournal.com/ask-annika/sorenstam-clubs-mental-game-swedish-food/
28. Burton, E. (2018). *The civility project: How to build a culture of reverence to improve wellness, productivity and profit*. Bowker Identifier Services.
29. Locke, E. A. (1968). Toward a theory of task motivation and incentives. *Organizational Behavior and Performances*, 3(2), 157–189. https://doi.org/10.1016/0030-5073(68)90004-4
30. Locke, E. A., Shaw, K. N., Saari, L. M., & Latham, G. P. (1981). Goal setting and task performance: 172–173. *Psychological Bulletin*, 90(1), 125–152. https://doi.org/10.1037/0033-2909.90.1.125
31. Locke, E. A., & Latham, G. P. (2002). Building a practically useful theory of goal setting and task motivation: A 35-year odyssey. *American Psychologist*, 57(9), 705–717. https://doi.org/10.1037/0003-066X.57.9.705
32. Höchli, B., Brügger, A., & Messner, C. (2018). How focusing on superordinate goals motivates broad, long-term goal pursuit: A theoretical perspective. *Frontiers in Psychology*, 9, 1879. https://doi.org/10.3389/fpsyg.2018.01879

Notes to Module 6

33. Church, D.; Yount, G., Brooks, A. J. (2012). The Effect of Emotional Freedom Techniques on Stress Biochemistry. *The Journal of nervous and mental disease* 200(10):891-6 https://doi.org/10.1097/NMD.0b013e31826b9fc1
34. Adapted from https://www.thetappingsolution.com/
35. Bach, D., Groesbeck, G., Stapleton, P., Sims, R., Blickheuser, K., & Church, D. (2019). Clinical EFT (Emotional Freedom Techniques) improves multiple physiological markers of health. *Journal of Evidence-Based Integrative Medicine*, 24. https://doi.org/10.1177/2515690X18823691
36. Church, D., Stapleton, P., Sabot, D. (2020). App-based delivery of clinical emotional freedom techniques: Cross-sectional study of app user self-ratings. *JMIR mHealth and uHealth*, 8(10). https://doi.org/10.2196/18545
37. Ortner, N. (2017). *The tapping solution for manifesting your greatest self: 21 days to releasing self-doubt, cultivating inner peace, and creating a life you love*. Hay House Inc.
38. Church, D. (2020). *Bliss brain: The neuroscience of remodeling your brain for resilience, creativity, and joy*. Hay House Inc.
39. Church, D. (2018). *Mind to matter: The astonishing science of how your brain creates material reality*. Hay House Inc.
40. Yale Happiness Course https://www.cnn.com/2020/03/23/health/yale-happiness-course-wellness/index.html
41. Hughes, W. G. (1982). Guided imagery training as treatment for alcoholism.

[Master's thesis, University of Florida] *George A. Smathers Libraries.* https://www.ebooksread.com/authors-eng/william-gordon-hughes/guided-imagery-training-as-treatment-for-alcoholism-hgu.shtml.

42. Miller, L., Balodis, I. M., McClintock, C. H., Xu, J., Lacadie, C. M., Sinha, R., & Potenza, M. N. (2019). Neural correlates of personalized spiritual experiences. *Cerebral Cortex*, 29(6), 2331–2338. https://doi.org/10.1093/cercor/bhy102

43. McClintock, C. H., Worhunsky, P. D., Xu, J., Balodis, I., Sinha, R, Miller, L., & Potenza, M. N. (2019). Spiritual experiences are related to engagement of a ventral frontotemporal functional brain network: Implications for prevention and treatment of behavioral and substance addictions. *Journal of Behavioral Addictions* 8(4), 678–691. https://doi.org/10.1556/2006.8.2019.71

Notes to Module 7

44. Beck, J. S. (2011). *Cognitive therapy: Basics and beyond* (2nd ed.). Guilford Press.

45. Josefowitz, N. (2017). Incorporating imagery into thought records: Increasing engagement in balanced thoughts. *Cognitive and Behavioral Practice*, 24(1), 90–100. https://doi.org/10.1016/j.cbpra.2016.03.005

46. Fritz, R. (1984). *The path of least resistance: Principles for creating what you want to create.* DMA.

47. Locke, E. A., & Latham, G. P. (2019). The development of goal setting theory: A half century retrospective. *Motivation Science*, 5(2), 93–105. https://doi.org/10.1037/mot0000127

48. Hagura, N., Haggard, P., & Diedrichsen, J. (2017). Perceptual decisions are biased by the cost to act. *eLife*, 6, Article Number 18422. https://doi.org/10.7554/eLife.18422

Notes to Module 8

49. Achterberg, J. (1984). Imagery and medicine: Psychophysiological speculations. *Journal of Mental Imagery*, 8(4), 1–13. https://psycnet.apa.org/record/1986-03196-001

50. Chen, S. F., Wang, H. H., Yang, H. Y., & Chung, U. L. (2015). Effect of relaxation with guided imagery on the physical and psychological symptoms of breast cancer patients undergoing chemotherapy. *Iranian Red Crescent Medical Journal*, 17(11). https://doi.org/10.5812/ircmj.31277

51. Coelho, A., Parola, V., Sandgren, A., Fernandes, O., Kolcaba, K., & Apóstolo, J. (2018). The effects of guided imagery on comfort in palliative care. *Journal of Hospice & Palliative Nursing*, 20(4), 392–399. https://doi.org/10.1097/NJH.0000000000000460

52. Simonton, O.C., Matthews-Simonton, S., Creighton, J. (1978). *Getting Well Again: A Step-By-Step Self-Help Guide to Overcoming Cancer for Patients and Their Families.* J P Tarcher, Inc.

53. Rossman, M. L. (2002). Imagery: The body's natural language for

healing. *Alternative Therapies, 8*(1). https://pubmed.ncbi.nlm.nih.gov/11795626/
54. Leviton, C. D. (2004). What is guided imagery? The cutting-edge process in mind/body medical procedures. *Annals of the American Psychotherapy Association, 7*(2), 22–29.
55. Hamilton, J., Fawson, S., May, J., Andrade, J., & Kavanagh, D. J. (2013). Brief guided imagery and body scanning interventions reduce food cravings. *Appetite, 71,* 158–162. https://doi.org/10.1016/j.appet.2013.08.005
56. May, J., Kavanagh, D. J., & Andrade, J. (2015). The elaborated intrusion theory of desire: A 10-year retrospective and implications for addiction treatments. *Addictive Behaviors, 44,* 29–34. https://doi.org/10.1016/j.addbeh.2014.09.016
57. Spaid, W. M. (2004). The use of guided imagery for cocaine abuse. *Journal of Evidence-Based Social Work, 1*(4), 83–96. https://doi.org/10.1300/J394v01n04_05
58. Walker, L. G., Walker, M. B., Ogston, K., Heys, S. D., Ah-See, A. K., Miller, I. D., Hutcheon, A. W., Sarkar, T. K., & Eremin, O. (1999). Psychological, clinical and pathological effects of relaxation training and guided imagery during primary chemotherapy. *British Journal of Cancer, 80,* 262–268. https://doi.org/10.1038/sj.bjc.6690349
59. León-Pizarro, C., Gich, I., Barthe, E., Rovirosa, A., Farrús, B., Casas, F., Verger, E., Biete, A., Craven-Bartle, J., Sierra, J., and Arcusa, A. (2007). A randomized trial of the effect of training in relaxation and guided imagery techniques in improving psychological and quality-of-life indices for gynecologic and breast brachytherapy patients. *Psycho-Oncology, 16*(11), 971–979. https://doi.org/10.1002/pon.1171
60. Halpin, L. S., Speir, A. M., CapoBianco, P., Barnett, S. D. (2002). Guided imagery in cardiac surgery. *Outcomes Management, 6*(3), 132–137. https://pubmed.ncbi.nlm.nih.gov/12134377
61. Parizad, N., Goli, R., Faraji, N., Mam-Qaderi, M., Mirzaee, R., Gharebaghi, N., Baghaie, R., Feizipour, H., Haghighi, M. M. (2021). Effect of guided imagery on anxiety, muscle pain, and vital signs in patients with COVID-19: A randomized controlled trial. *Complementary Therapies in Clinical Practice, 43,* Article Number 101335. https://doi.org/10.1016/j.ctcp.2021.101335

Notes to Module 9
62. Sheldon, K. M., & Lyubomirsky, S. (2006). How to increase and sustain positive emotion: The effects of expressing gratitude and visualizing best possible selves. *The Journal of Positive Psychology, 1*(2), 73–82. https://doi.org/10.1080/17439760500510676
63. Lotze, M., & Halsband, U. (2006). Motor imagery. *Journal of*

    Physiology-Paris, 99(4–6), 386–395. https://doi.org/10.1016/j.jphysparis.2006.03.012

64. Munzert, J., Lorey, B., & Zentgraf, K. (2009). Cognitive motor processes: The role of motor imagery in the study of motor representations. *Brain Research Reviews, 60*(2), 306–326. https://doi.org/10.1016/j.brainresrev.2008.12.024
65. Byers, T. (2019, February 7). *The power of the mind through visualization.* Swimming World Magazine. https://www.swimmingworldmagazine.com/news/the-power-of-the-mind-through-visualization/
66. Gallo, C. (2016, May 24). *3 daily habits of peak performers, according to Michael Phelps' coach.* Forbes. https://www.forbes.com/sites/carminegallo/2016/05/24/3-daily-habits-of-peak-performers-according-to-michael-phelps-coach/
67. Toth, A. J., McNeill, E., Hayes, K., Moran, A. P., & Campbell, M. (2020). Does mental practice still enhance performance? A 24 year follow-up and meta-analytic replication and extension. *Psychology of Sport and Exercise, 48,* Article Number 101672. https://doi.org/10.1016/j.psychsport.2020.101672
68. Simonsmeier, B. A., Andronie, M., Buecker, S., & Frank, C. (2020). The effects of imagery interventions in sports: A meta-analysis. *International Review of Sport and Exercise Psychology, 1–22.* https://doi.org/10.1080/1750984X.2020.1780627
69. Paravlic, A. H., Slimani, M., Tod, D., Marusic, U., Milanovic, Z., & Pisot, R. (2018). Effects and dose-response relationships of motor imagery practice on strength development in healthy adult populations: A systematic review and meta-analysis. *Sports Med, 48,* 1165–1187. https://doi.org/10.1007/s40279-018-0874-8
70. Jesmy, J., & Joseph, M. M. (2018). Imagery: It's effects and benefits on sports performance and psychological variables: A review study. *International Journal of Physiology, Nutrition, and Physical Education, 3*(2), 190–193. [sic]

Notes to Module 10

71. Archer, D. W. (1991). *Thoughts for a greater Detroit* [Unpublished pamphlet].
72. Archer, D. & Neely, A. D. (2001). *Detroit: Building on a solid foundation a community vision for 2002–2010* [Unpublished pamphlet].
73. Archer, D. W. (1993). *A vision and strategy for city wide revitalization* [Unpublished pamphlet].

Made in the USA
Columbia, SC
01 February 2022